At Home, At Sea

W9-CHQ-959

Developmental Editing, Text and Cover Design: Dana Degenhardt
Photography: Frank Chillemi (except as indicated in Photo Credits on page 229).
Postcard Design: Kim Palermo, Elm St Printing, Camden, ME
Printed in the United States of America by Bookmasters, Inc., Mansfield, Ohio

Printed on recycled paper with vegetable dyes

Excerpt from **Under Sail, The Dredgeboats of Delaware Bay** by Donald H. Rolfs reprinted with permission from the Wheaton Historical Association, Millville, NJ.

Composting at Sea article reprinted with permission from Maine Businesses for Social Responsibility (MEBSR), Portland, ME.

At Home, At Sea Copyright © 2004 Baggywrinkle Publishing
All rights reserved. No part of this book may be reproduced without written permission from the publisher, except by a reviewer who may quote brief passages or reproduce illustrations in a review with appropriate credits; nor may any part of this book be reproduced, stored in a retrieval system, or transmitted in any form or by any means – electronic, mechanical, photocopying, recording, or other without written permission from the publisher.

Member, Maine Businesses for Social Responsibility (MEBSR)
http://www.mebsr.org/

ISBN 0-9749706-0-3
Library of Congress Control Number: 2004090788

First Edition
May 2004

For more information on the *J.&E. Riggin*, visit our website at
www.mainewindjammer.com
or email us at
info@riggin.com

For more information or to order **At Home, At Sea**, visit
www.AtHomeAtSea.com
or email us at
info@AtHomeAtSea.com

Or call us at 800 869-0604

At Home, At Sea

Recipes from the Maine Windjammer

J.&E. Riggin

Anne Mahle

Dedications

To my Mom and Dad for such
a great beginning.

To Jon – my husband, best friend,
partner and co-parent. My heart is big
for you.

Table of Contents

Introduction

The subtle sounds of nature and the sea. The easy companionship of new and old friends. The simple pleasures of delicious meals prepared and served with passion and care. From May to October each year, this is our life on our Maine windjammer *J.&E. Riggin.*

I've worked on ships nearly 15 years and have been lucky to combine my love of the sea and my passion for cooking. Together with my husband, Captain Jon Finger, we take as many as 24 passengers out for weeklong cruises among the pristine islands of Penobscot Bay. For our passengers, a week on the *Riggin* revolves around the sun, the tides, the fellow shipmates and crew of this historic schooner. And the food – made fresh each day in our galley – steamed lobster, warm bread fresh from the woodstove, and meals made from the bounty of locally grown vegetables and fruits picked at their peak.

If you aren't able to join us for a week of sailing and delicious meals, then this book is the next best thing. I serve many of these dishes on board (returning passengers often ask for particular favorites) while there are also family favorites from our winters ashore. I've also

included a number of recipes shared among the past and present cooks from other windjammers, and recipes passed down from my Mom and Grandma. Since I'm not expecting you to have a woodstove tucked away in your kitchen, or to be cooking for 30 people at a time, I've scaled these recipes down (most serve 4-6 people) and tested them on my trusty GE gas stove at home.

More than a cookbook

I wanted to offer more than a cookbook; I also wanted to give you a taste of life on our much-loved *Riggin*. So I've added some special features in this book you won't normally find in a cookbook, including:

✳ *Our Story* – How we came to our stewardship of the *Riggin*, a National Historic Landmark – and my experiences working my way up from mess cook to cook on our own windjammer.

✳ *A Week at Sea* – Menus and highlights of a typical week on the *Riggin*, with color pictures by award-winning photographer Frank Chillemi.

✳ *Lobster Bake* – Our weekly steamed lobster dinners (with all the fixin's) on the shore of one of the hundreds of Maine's beautiful islands.

✳ *Vignettes* – Slices of shipboard life, stories of our passengers and family, as well as cooking tips and shortcuts.

✳ *Social Responsibility* – Our efforts as small business owners to preserve our planet and give back to our community. This is our choice, our lifestyle, and we want to share how we make it work.

✳ *Dietary Index and Local Sources* – In addition, in the back of this book you'll find a listing of recipes in this book that are low-fat, low-carbohydrate, or vegetarian, as well as a list of my favorite local food sources.

Acknowledgements

The idea for this cookbook began almost from the day we bought the *J.&E. Riggin*; but dreaming and doing are two very different things. I knew that when the time was right, the right partners for this book would present themselves – and I wasn't wrong. Frank Chillemi, a passenger who just happens to be an award-winning photographer, has been leading photography cruises on the *Riggin* for the past several years. Frank offered to take the pictures for the cookbook and I couldn't be more grateful; his skill and passion for photography helped create this book. Dana Degenhardt is the other member of the team. She's been a project manager specializing in books and software packages and is also a Culinary Institute of America graduate. She loves to do all the things I hate – edit, design, futz, details, details, details. This book wouldn't be half as good without her input.

Throughout my cooking and sailing life, two people have been my mentors. Ellen Barnes, my boss on the first windjammer I ever worked on, taught me to not just talk but to *do*. She and her husband, Ken Barnes, have watched me become a grownup, a wife, a business owner and a parent. Her advice has been refreshing, honest and invaluable. Hans Bucher, Chef/Owner at Jessica's Restaurant taught me how to make food taste good *all* the time. The rare camaraderie we shared working side by side in a small, hot kitchen will always be treasured.

Thanks also to my mess cooks and nannies over the years who have supported this work and taken such good care of our girls while I'm cooking. Finally, thanks to our passengers on the *J.&E. Riggin:* without their insistence, I would have never put fingertips to keyboard.

Our Story

I believe in food cooked with the freshest ingredients; using my hands to shape bread; taking time and care when I'm cooking; and sitting at the table with friends and family and sharing the soul-filled food we've created. I love the smell, shape, feel and look of pure ingredients. I want to teach my daughters by example that the most precious and sacred time of the day is dinnertime, when we come together at the close of our days with loved ones to share, discuss, argue and agree. To me, this is true nourishment. While "fast food" may be convenient, fully nourishing ourselves is more than simply removing the empty feeling in our bellies. Food is a way that we can connect – to our families and to nature.

This wasn't always the way I thought about food and cooking. I came to it by a roundabout way – falling in love with sailing, Maine, and my husband and co-owner of the *Riggin*, Captain Jon Finger.

How it started, or "Not the Navy Blue Suit, Thank You"

Before I came to Maine, working in restaurants was a way for me to earn money, not a passion. My first jobs were in the kitchens of restaurants, but they weren't places where the craft and the passion of good food was evident – anywhere. I couldn't say that I was proud of the ingredients going into what I was making or, obviously, the final product. Most of it was food made on a large scale for huge numbers of people and presented in a way that did nothing to enhance the dining experience.

Working my way through college in kitchens I wasn't proud of, I arrived at my senior year at Michigan State University about to graduate with a B.S. in Psychology. Everyone kept telling me that I couldn't "do" anything with only an undergraduate degree in Psychology and my glib response was always that I would get an advanced degree. But by the time I was into my senior year of college, I knew that I could not stomach one more second of school much less the four more years required to get a PhD.

So I had the brilliant idea to "take a year off." I decided I wanted to travel, and I wanted to learn how to sail, and I needed to make enough money so that I wouldn't have to call home. Why travel? Save a brief summer in Europe, I'd only lived in the Midwest – I wanted to experience something different. Why sailing? Again it was different, outside, different, physical and different.

A few weeks before I graduated from college, needing a job, I met the daughter of the owners of the Schooner *Stephen Taber*, a Maine windjammer. With the realization that I could actually get *paid* to sail, I called about a job in the Maine windjammer fleet. I talked with Ellen Barnes, co-owner and Cook on the *Taber;* she said if I could be in Rockland, Maine the day after I graduated, I had a job as a Mess Cook. Wahoo! I was so excited I got off the phone before asking how much the job paid, or even what a Mess Cook was. Ellen's daughter and I got up at 4am (I was *much* more accustomed to getting to sleep around 4am) and drove 16 hours from Michigan to Maine. I got up again at the same unearthly hour the next day and started my first day as Mess Cook.

I found out quickly that a Mess Cook is aptly named. I cleaned up after the mess maker, the cook, all summer long. Amid all of the chopping and cleaning, I learned

– about baking from scratch, slow-cooked food and woodstoves. This was my first exposure to the real craft of creating soulful food - food made with pride, good ingredients, time, thoughtfulness and care.

My plan that year was to sail for one summer, then get a real job, something 9 to 5 where I'd be wearing a navy blue suit, and start working toward a PhD.... The next year, my plan was to sail for two summers and **then** get a real job, something 9 to 5 where I'd be wearing a navy blue suit. Never happened. I'd fallen in love with sailing, Maine, and Jon Finger.

Jon was also from the Midwest; he grew up right next to Lake Michigan and spent his summers sailing. He paid one dollar for his first boat, which was missing sails, a rudder and other unimportant items – all of which he fabricated. When he was sixteen he had his first sail on a windjammer; from then on he knew he wanted to be a captain of one of these majestic vessels. After 4 years in the Coast Guard, two of those on the U.S. Barque Eagle (our ambassador ship for the United States), he came to Maine and the windjammer fleet. He spent the next ten years working for other captains in the fleet, in Bermuda on a research vessel, and running his own daysailer.

My first glimpse of Jon was my first morning in the galley, as he peered at me over the watermelon that he was balancing precariously on top of an armload of boxed groceries. It wasn't the last I'd see of him. Whenever I had a break, I'd sneak back to the quarterdeck and get him to teach me something about sailing. While later I'd become passionate about cooking, when I was a mess cook it was a means to an end. I really wanted to learn how to sail and so spent every available second on deck. We are a perfect example of opposites attracting. I am loud, lively, busy, talkative and laugh a lot. Jon is calm, steady, thoughtful, quiet and kind – a perfect captain. While we tried to keep our interest in each other a secret, it's hard to do in such a small community! It was obvious to both of us very early on that our relationship was different and that we wanted to build a life and grow older and wiser together.

The following summer I became a deck hand on the *Taber* while Jon moved on to run his own friendship sloop *Grace O'Malley* as a daysailer. After spending that one summer apart, we realized that we really liked being together far more than we did being apart. We also realized that while we wanted to work on the same ship, we needed to have separate areas of responsibility. So I chose to move back into the galley. By this time I had discovered that this really was no sacrifice as I could come up on deck and do all of the fun deck stuff, like driving the yawl boat, hauling on sails and tacking, but if the weather became cold and rainy, all of a sudden I would need to "check my pies" in the galley by the warm, dry stove.

The Craft of Cooking

After three summers in the fleet – one year as mess cook, one as deckhand and one as head cook on the *Victory Chimes* – I decided I wanted to learn more about the craft and the art of cooking. While I'd been cooking for several years, I knew there was a

lot more I didn't know, like how to correct a dish if something untoward happened. What if I forgot about the bread rising since early morning and it looked like Jabba the Hut? I needed to learn the why of cooking and I found that at Jessica's European Bistro.

Jessica's was the best restaurant in the area and our favorite. After two interviews, numerous phone calls and an offer to work for free, Hans Bucher hired me as Sous Chef and quickly became my mentor. The time spent under Hans' tutelage taught me traditional European-style cooking. I learned about the delight of making food taste and look good all of the time. Hans was a Swiss-trained chef and the youngest executive chef at the Hyatt when he first came to the U.S. He was Swiss-German; I was of German descent, so sometimes we butted heads! Hans liked to listen to country music. All. Day. Long. After a time, I became not only tolerant, but a fan. So much so that when I first left Jessica's, I couldn't cook without country music playing in the background.

It was during this time that Jon and I married. Bagpipes skirling, we were piped into an outdoor chapel and married by Captains Ken and Ellen Barnes – the people who had first introduced us. After the ceremony, we had a champagne toast on the

Victory Chimes and a reception catered by Hans at our house. People still tell us it was the most special wedding they've ever attended.

I spent three years under Hans' tutelage. After a time, adventure beckoned, and Jon and I headed south. We were hired as Captain and Chef for a yacht owned by a retired New York Trust banker, spending the summers in New England and the winters in the Caribbean. It would be our job to take out either the owner or charter guests for weeklong trips.

Working on a private yacht is about as far away from Maine windjammers as a person can get and still be sailing. I was cooking for a maximum of four passengers, so I had wonderful opportunities to be creative. I also had to learn to fold towels so neatly and uniformly that Martha Stewart would have been put to shame.

What I loved most about the tropical islands of the Caribbean was shopping in the local markets for fruits, vegetables and spices. The local women peddling their produce were always a highlight of my week. I also enjoyed the challenge of planning menus around the dietary needs and preferences of our passengers; I liked it best if I could meet the folks when they boarded and then decided what I would cook for them. It was a real treat to be able to tailor the meals to suit the small group on board. This is where I developed a Caribbean influence in my cooking, using more fruits and salsas.

Every summer Jon and I would bring the yacht up to Maine to charter during the month of August. We would invariably arrive at night, but we always knew when we'd gotten home – we could smell the pine trees. We would stand on deck with our heads thrown back looking up at the cacophony of stars and take big gulps of the fragrance of pine.

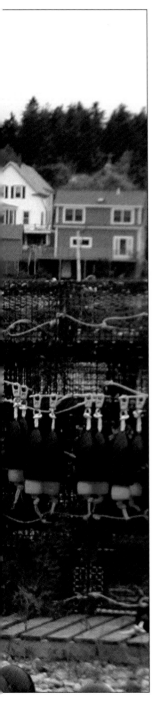

Sometimes the yachting world seems more romantic than it really is. After dusting electrical panels with dental picks, cleaning toilets with toothbrushes and polishing engine blocks until they shone like mirrors, we longed for the simplicity of Maine. Three years in the lucrative yachting business allowed us the freedom to return home to Maine, where our hearts live, and buy or start a business. Jon tells the story of driving all the way from Indiana to Maine for the first time. When he stepped out of the car and breathed in, he knew he'd found the place where his heart was most full. I feel the same. I feel less encumbered in Maine than I do anywhere else I've ever traveled or lived.

We briefly considered and discarded a restaurant, a bed and breakfast, and a bakery; while all were interesting, only a Maine windjammer allowed us to work together and more importantly raise our family together, as by this time I was pregnant with our first child, Chlöe.

Would you like some schooner with your coffee?

On a crisp September Saturday in 1997 Jon found Dave Allen, then the owner of the *J.&E. Riggin*, changing the oil in the schooner's 20 year-old yawl boat. Yawl boats are beautiful wooden workboats for vessels without inboard engines (as is the case with many boats in the fleet). They serve as a tugboat for moving the vessels in and out of tight harbors, and as a shuttle to get folks ashore. Dave was grunting (and swearing) with bloody knuckles and oil running down his arm from wrist to elbow as he held the greasy oil filter up for inspection. Dave, only half joking, asked Jon if he wanted to buy a schooner. Jon, not joking at all, said yes. Off to breakfast they went to agree on a price.

Two months later we bought ourselves the *J.&E. Riggin*. Below is an excerpt about her from **Under Sail, The Dredgeboats of Delaware Bay** by Donald H. Rolfs.

Undoubtedly, the most legendary schooner that ever sailed the bay was the *J.&E. Riggin*. This dredgeboat was 76 feet, 4 inches long with a 22 foot, 3 inch beam. The *J.&E.* was polish [sic] rigged and carried 4,000 square feet of canvas. Captain Ed Riggin involuntarily glows from stem to stern as he relates the exploits of the grand old boat. "My gosh," he said, "it was almost as if she was a live creature a – risin' up out o' the sea, runnin' before the wind, a-goin' wing and wing. I would have to climb up on top of the wheel box to see where I was goin'. You know, she was never beat in a race. Many of the 'old gents' thought they could take her but nobody ever did. Sunday afternoons they used to wait for us at the mouth of the river to give her a try, but there weren't nobody could ever take her."

Captain Frank Hinson concurred with Captain Riggin's estimation of the *J.&E.* "I believe it was the way she was rigged up," said Captain Frank. "She was hung just right. We were comin' down the bay one day and I had the *Richord Lore [sic]*, an old time boat, pushin' down with the yawlboat...there wasn't a bit of wind, not a bit, to plant... looked up and here come the *J.&E. Riggin* down the bay. She was comin' on so fast we thought she was pushin' with her yawlboat. She went by us and didn't even have her yawlboat down! She had a line from her main boom to the rigging on one side and a line from her fore boom to the rigging on the other side... had her wung out... and that thing was a-goin' down the bay just the same as us. Yep, she was hung just exactly right... take a little breeze of wind and you would just have to reef her down to nothing to hold her dredges on the bottom."

Neal Parent

The *J.&E. Riggin* is still a beautiful schooner and although she's still fast, she doesn't carry oysters anymore, she carries passengers. She was built as an oystering schooner in 1927 in Dorchester, New Jersey on the Morris River. Charles Riggin, a fisherman, had her built and named her after his two sons Jacob and Edward. She gained a fine reputation in the Delaware

Bay as an able sailor, winning the only Oyster Schooner Race ever held in 1929. She was designated a National Historic Landmark in 1991.

After only four owners, Dave and Sue Allen bought her in 1974 and over three years converted her into a passenger vessel. They owned the boat for twenty-four years before selling her to Jon and me in 1998.

Baby on Board: Our First Season

Some might argue that buying a business and having a baby all in one year would be crazy and we would agree. But we did it. We successfully managed to sail with nearly a full complement of passengers our first season and were lucky enough to have Chlöe, a happy baby girl who just liked to be close to Mama or Papa.

Some might also argue that you never buy something without test-driving it first and, again, we would agree. Nevertheless, our first sail on the *Riggin* was the day we left the dock with our first group of passengers. This is not quite as strange as it seems; by the time we bought the *Riggin*, we knew all the boats in the fleet and how they sailed. Still it was a bit of a surprise to a passenger on our first trip out when he asked Jon how long we'd been sailing the *Riggin*. Jon looked at his watch and said, with his usual straight-guy face, "Oh, about 2 hours." The passenger was a trifle surprised

Baby Soup

When Chlöe was two, she liked to sit in the galley and help with dishes. As anyone who has experienced a two-year-old close to water knows, "help" is the last thing you need if you care about being done with dishes in this century. "Baby Soup" was what we played instead. She'd sit in the big stew pot and we'd "season" her with salt, pepper and spices and stir with the long wooden spoon (of course, this was always the last pot washed). Later this turned into a deck game where we'd give both girls (Ella, now 3 and Chlöe, 6) Dixie cups of spices and herbs, some kitchen utensils and a deck bucket of salt water.

Low Rider

Our nickname in the fleet is "Low Rider" because our hull is sleek and low to the water. During the summer we will often anchor together for festivals and raftups (when all the boats tie up side by side); occasionally the crews of each boat play pranks on each other. We found this license plate on our transom one morning after we were all anchored together. There was a pair of "fuzzy dice" hanging off the bowsprit as well.

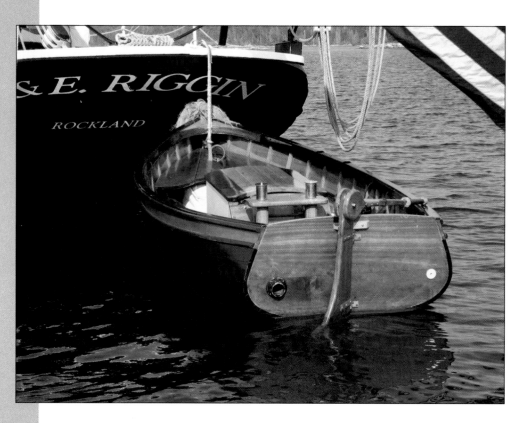

by Jon's response – Jon was so comfortable at the wheel the passenger assumed he'd been doing it for years!

Making our Mark

We've now owned the *J.&E. Riggin* since 1998. Jon and I don't really view it as ownership, but rather stewardship. This is our tenure. We will eventually pass this National Historic Landmark, a beautiful example of our collective American history, on to another. What makes the *Riggin* ours during our tenure are the special touches that we bring to her.

Food –

It's impossible to make a dish any better than the ingredients you start with, which is why the herbs and fresh vegetables that we grow are so integral to our food. One of the things I love about getting different vegetables and fruits every week is the creativity that these beautiful products inspire. People often ask if the menu is the same every week and while it would sure make my life easier if it were, I adjust the menu to what is fresh from the farm that week.

I am constantly striving to take advantage of the special brand of heat I cook with on board, my woodstove. It's the same wonderful heat that folks all over the country are recreating by building wood-fired brick ovens. The foods that work best in a woodstove are roasts and stews like Black Forest Pork Stew, breads like Caramelized Onion Bread and pies - anything that lends itself to slow cooking. Anything that could benefit from the smoky flavor of wood heat.

Music –

Music on boats is somewhat of a tradition. Without the entertainments of modern life that can sometimes separate us from our neighbors, we find ourselves entertaining each other in the way our ancestors did – with our voices and instruments like the guitar or penny whistle. The acoustics of sound on the water seems to add a purity to the notes and is an enchanting way to end our day. Four years under the tutelage of folk musicians Cindy Kallet and David Dodson allow us to entertain our guests with folk songs of humor and whimsy. And we're often pleasantly surprised at the number of talented passengers who share their music with us.

Social Responsibility –

A few years into owning the *J.&E. Riggin*, we made a commitment to the process of social responsibility. I say process, because we are constantly balancing social choices with fiscal choices. The most important thing we need to remember is that if we are not fiscally responsible and making a profit, we won't be able to make good choices for the environment or our employees because we won't be in business.

In the beginning, we started with things that cost us nothing but made an impact in some way.

Recycling and composting became our first goal. We had so much organic matter going into the municipal dump – now it feeds our healthy 1000 square foot garden. We reduced the amount of garbage on board from 2-3 bags a day to 2-3 bags a **week**.

Our next goal was to find effective and safe cleaning products that didn't pollute the very waters on which we sailed. It was equally important to maintain a very high level of sanitation. What is interesting is that we found we saved a good deal of money by making our own cleaning supplies. We also found that the ones we now use are as effective if not more effective than the brand-name products we used before. The recipes we use are in the section entitled "Eco-Friendly Cleaning." Two books that I found very helpful when developing the recipes that work on the boat were *Clean and Green* by Annie Berthold-Bond and *Clean House, Clean Planet* by Karen Logan. While we haven't found natural alternatives to every product we need to use on the boat, we have seriously reduced the number and amount of non-natural products we use.

Our commitment to buying local produce is one of our stronger decisions and is a cornerstone of my cooking. There are some practical limitations as Maine's growing season is short and limited, so we supplement what we can't get from our Community Supported Farm at the local grocery store.

We have also made a conscious decision to support our community. Again, we started slowly, doing what we could, donating what we could. Every business has to start somewhere. This isn't about having an absolutely pristine record from your first day in business, but is more about the striving to make conscious, responsible decisions. We now give 5% of our profits to kids, education or the environment.

Family Business

Our family is an important aspect of our business - we chose to own a Maine windjammer because we could raise our children together on board. Interestingly, the *Riggin* started as a family-run business. Charles Riggin, the builder and first owner named her after his sons Jacob and Edward. Over the next two decades, the boys and their father took turns at the helm oystering off the coast of New Jersey.

We are now lucky enough to be following in Charles Riggin's footsteps, able to raise our daughters in such a unique way. It is our pleasure to be able to share our family with the folks that come on board and we feel we go sailing with 24 friends and family members every week.

General recipe notes

There are two kinds of people who create good food for a living: cooks and bakers. If you are a cook, you see recipes as guidelines and something to easily change.

Baby as Chart Weight

Ella was one of those babies that you could plop down and she would be happy just looking around. The place I used to plop her was the navigation station (where the charts and compass are) right in front of Jon. She ended up acting as a chart weight to keep the charts from blowing away. She'd watch the wheel turn, the GPS screen change and the flags flying. Now of course, she doesn't sit still long enough for any of that!

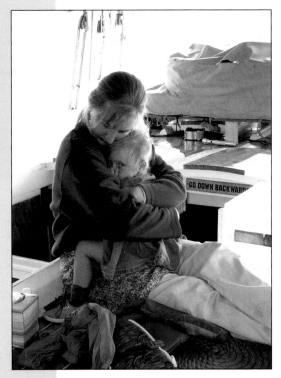

You are not a rule follower! If you are a baker at heart, then recipes are a formula to follow to the letter. I am the former and have a really hard time doing the latter. So it is in the spirit of creativity and fun that I encourage you to use these recipes as a starting point – and why I've made some of them with all sorts of variations on a theme. Don't worry though if you don't happen to have a woodstove handy at home. All of these recipes have been tested in a home kitchen. With that in mind, there are a few points I want to mention before you move on to the recipes.

※　All the yeast breads have instructions for making the bread with a bread machine. The bread machine recipes were tested in both Zojirushi and Wellbuilt machines. They are made for a two pound loaf. If your machine is only a $1\,^1/_2$ pound machine, reduce the amounts by $^1/_3$.

※　I don't proof my yeast as I use it all of the time. This is why the yeast is added to the dry ingredients and mixed briefly rather than being combined with warm liquid first. It just saves a step. If you use your yeast every six months, or can't remember the last time you did use it, then proof it by adding it to 1 cup of warm water. If it bubbles after a minute or so, it's fine.

* I always use large eggs in a recipe.
* I have access to an abundance of fresh herbs from my garden, so most of these recipes call for fresh herbs If you don't have fresh herbs you can substitute dried herbs. A good rule of thumb is to cut the amount in half if you're substituting dry herbs.
* When a recipe has an ingredient that is used at two or more separate times during preparation it will be listed more than once, in the order in which it will be used.
* When cooking beef, the USDA says it's safest to cook the meat to an internal resting temperature of 145°.
* I've added a number of helpful suggestions and comments throughout the recipes. You'll find them in margin of the recipes or the beginning of a chapter.

Breakfast & Brunch

It's early morning, my favorite time of day. Everything is quiet; half the summer it's still dark. In late summer, I can even see Orion in the eastern sky heralding the fall. My day on board starts at 4:30 am when I wake to light the woodstove. I often watch the sun peek over the horizon in a cascade of colors – reds, blues, orange, purple – sometimes alone, sometimes joined by an equally appreciative passenger. The deckhands poke their heads up on deck. The lanterns, set out for those nocturnal nature calls, are blown out and the morning dew wiped from the topsides. My mess cook rises and rubs the fairy dust from her/his eyes and begins the chopping and coffee making for the day. A counterpoint to the gentle wakening of the passengers and crew, this is my busiest time of day. By this time, I'm well into my baking so that all the baking is done before breakfast: hopefully the better part of my cooking, as well. It's at these times when I think I should wear an apron that says: "Hang on – I'm measuring!"

The rich aromas of wood smoke and our own special blend of Rock City Roasters coffee greet our guests as they rise to take their first cup of coffee, tea or cocoa on deck. The smell of sizzling bacon, or granola roasting in the oven, follow. As more passengers rise for the day, the sounds of soft laughter and camaraderie mix with the sounds of nature. The air is crisp and bright or maybe misty with a morning fog that has yet to burn off.

For breakfast our guests might be treated to jam with fresh biscuits, farm raised eggs and sausage made by our local butcher. I try to alternate my breakfasts between the hearty and the healthy: Maine blueberry or banana pancakes, butcher's cut bacon and melon wedges one morning, Apricot Coffee Cake, homemade Granola and all the accompaniments the next.

Apricot Coffee Cake

Makes 9 servings

"One Ringie-Dingie..."

The ringing of bells on board ships has been a tradition from the earliest days of sail. Bells are used for signaling, keeping time, raising the alarm and, more recently, calling everyone to meals. The ringing of the ship's bell for meals is a tradition we keep on the J.&E. Riggin.

The system is based on the four-hour watch typical on naval vessels. The watches run from 8-12, 12-4 and 4-8. A bell is struck once at the end of the first half hour of a four-hour watch, twice after the first hour, etc., until eight bells mark the end of the watch. We eat at 8 am, 12 noon and 6 pm, and therefore ring 8 bells, 8 bells and 4 bells.

Passengers often tell us that when they hear a bell after they've returned home, they automatically think it's time to eat!

If you double this recipe use a 9 x 13-inch pan.

Cake:

2 $\frac{1}{4}$ cups packed light brown sugar
$\frac{3}{4}$ cup (1$\frac{1}{2}$ sticks) softened butter
6 large eggs
1$\frac{1}{2}$ cups milk
4$\frac{1}{2}$ cups all-purpose flour
2 tablespoons baking powder
1$\frac{1}{2}$ teaspoons salt

Topping:

$\frac{1}{4}$ cup ($\frac{1}{2}$ stick) butter
$\frac{1}{2}$ cup brown sugar
$\frac{1}{2}$ cup all-purpose flour
$\frac{1}{2}$ cup chopped dried apricots

* Preheat oven to 350°. Grease a 9-inch square baking pan.
* In a large bowl, cream the butter and sugar.
* Mix in the eggs, then the milk.
* Sift in the flour, powder, and salt and mix until just blended.
* In a separate bowl blend the butter, brown sugar and flour with your fingers, then toss in the apricots.
* Place half the batter in the baking pan and sprinkle with half the topping. Repeat.
* Bake for 30 minutes, until a fork inserted in the center comes out clean.
* Cool in the pan and cut into squares.

Aunt Rita's Double Toffee Delight

Makes 24 squares

Topping:

1 1/2 cups packed light brown sugar
1 cup chopped nuts
1 tablespoon ground cinnamon

Cake:

1 cup all-purpose flour
1 cup sugar
2 teaspoons baking powder
1 teaspoon salt
1 cup water
3/4 cup vegetable oil
1 teaspoon vanilla extract
4 large eggs, lightly beaten
1 3.4-ounce package instant vanilla pudding mix
1 3.4-ounce package butterscotch pudding mix

✳ Preheat oven to 350°. Grease a 9 x 13-inch pan.

✳ Combine the topping ingredients in a medium bowl and set aside.

✳ Mix the dry ingredients in a large bowl.

✳ Add the water, oil, extract, eggs, and both pudding mixes and mix until just blended.

✳ Spread half of the batter into the greased pan and then cover with half of the brown sugar mixture.

✳ Add the remaining batter then the remaining brown sugar mixture.

✳ Bake for 40-45 minutes, until a fork inserted in the center comes out clean.

✳ Cool in the pan and cut into squares.

Blueberry Syrup

I make this on the boat with whatever berries or fruits are in season and serve it with French toast. It also makes a good dessert sauce.

2 cups fresh or frozen Maine blueberries
$^1/_2$ cup sugar
$^1/_2$ teaspoon vanilla extract

✴ Bring the berries and sugar to a boil in a medium saucepan.
✴ Reduce heat and simmer, uncovered, for 10 minutes.
✴ Remove from heat and add the vanilla.

Granola

Makes 12 cups

I often add dried fruit (raisins, pineapple cranberries) to the granola. If you do add dried fruit, don't bake it; stir it into the granola just *after* you've taken the granola out of the oven.

$^1/_2$ cup honey
$^3/_4$ cup vegetable oil
2 teaspoons pure vanilla extract
4 cups old-fashioned rolled oats
2 cups bran buds
$1^1/_2$ cups shredded coconut
$1^1/_2$ cups chopped walnuts

✴ Preheat oven to 250°.
✴ Put the honey, oil, and vanilla in a small pot; heat until warm.
✴ Mix the remaining ingredients together in a large bowl.
✴ Pour the honey mixture over the dry ingredients and toss thoroughly.
✴ Spread the granola evenly onto a large cookie pan (you may need two pans, depending on their size).
✴ Cook for 1 hour or until the mixture is golden brown, stirring once or twice.
✴ Cool completely and store in a Ziploc bag or airtight container.

Buttermilk Pancakes

1$^1/_2$ cups all-purpose flour
2 tablespoons sugar
1 teaspoon baking powder
$^1/_4$ teaspoon baking soda
$^1/_2$ teaspoon salt
1$^1/_3$ cups buttermilk
1 large egg
$^1/_4$ cup ($^1/_2$ stick) butter, melted and cooled
Additional butter for cooking

✳ In a large bowl, mix together the dry ingredients.

✳ Make a well in the flour mixture and mix in the buttermilk and egg.

✳ Stir in the butter.

✳ If you'd like, gently fold in any of the fruits or nuts in the variations listed below. Do not overmix.

✳ Heat a griddle or skillet over medium heat until hot, then add 1 tablespoon of butter. Pour or ladle the batter into the pan; when the pancakes start to set and you see bubbles popping on the pancakes, flip them and cook until the other side is brown.

✳ Keep the pancakes in a warm oven until all the pancakes are done.

Variations
Add 1$^1/_2$ cups blueberries, OR
1$^1/_2$ total cups chopped apples and walnuts (combined),
OR
1$^1/_2$ cups sliced bananas OR
Replace $^1/_2$ cup flour with $^1/_2$ cup oatmeal and add 1 cup
pumpkin puree

Crepes Eggs Benedict

This is a meal we have only once a year – Christmas morning. My mom started this tradition and Jon and I are carrying it on with our family in Maine. It's great if it's a family affair as you can assign jobs. There are so many eggs in this recipe that the cholesterol police will be unhappy, but it's so good, it's worth it. Once a year? Live a little!

Crepes:

$1\frac{1}{4}$ cups all-purpose flour
4 large eggs
1 cup milk
$1\frac{1}{4}$ cups cold water
3 tablespoons unsalted butter, melted
$\frac{1}{2}$ teaspoon salt
Butter for cooking

Hollandaise:

4 egg yolks
$\frac{1}{4}$ teaspoon salt
$\frac{1}{2}$ teaspoon dry mustard
1 tablespoon lemon juice
$\frac{1}{2}$ cup (1 stick) butter

For the rest:

8 eggs
8 slices Canadian bacon

Overall instructions:

❋ Make the crepe batter first (below) and put it in the fridge to rest for 30 minutes.
❋ While it's resting, make the Hollandaise (below) and set it in a warm water bath (I have put the blender container right into a pot of hot water on the stove and it hasn't leaked.)
❋ Warm the serving plates in the oven.
❋ Once the crepes are done resting, have one family member cook the crepes.
❋ When the crepes are nearly done, have another family member cook the Canadian bacon over medium-high heat (you are really just heating it up, so no need to go crazy here) and poach the eggs.
❋ Get an assembly line going to put the crepes together:
❋ Place a crepe on one of the warmed plates.

* Place the bacon in the center of the crepe, then the poached egg on the bacon.
* Fold both sides of the crepe over then gently roll the crepe over so the edges of the crepe are on the bottom. Repeat until all the eggs are gone then ladle the Hollandaise sauce over the crepes and serve.

Make the crepes:

* Mix the crepe ingredients at high speed in a blender or food processor for 30 seconds.
* Scrape down the sides and blend at least 30 seconds longer. Refrigerate for at least 30 minutes.
* Heat a small nonstick sauté pan over medium heat for 3 minutes.
* When it's hot, melt 1 teaspoon of butter and ladle $1/4$ cup crepe batter into the pan.
* Tilt the pan to coat the bottom and when you can see bubbles have formed, flip it.
* Place the finished crepes on a plate in a warm oven (Don't worry if the first crepe is a loss – it usually is – the next ones will be fine. You shouldn't need butter after the first crepe).

Make the Hollandaise:

This is my mom's recipe for Hollandaise and it works. Mom's Hollandaise is a bit more foolproof than the traditional method – easier on the arms, as well. You can use a whisk to combine all the ingredients – the Hollandaise ends up a bit fluffier but it's a bit trickier to do.

* Put the egg yolks, salt, mustard and lemon juice in blender. Cover and blend.
* Heat the butter until it is hot. Pour the butter into the running blender in a steady stream.
* Keep the Hollandaise warm over a hot water bath until you are ready to serve.

French Toast

I will use almost any leftover bread for this recipe. This is a good example of leftovers being better the second time around.

1 egg per person
$1/_2$ cup milk per person
1 teaspoon sugar
$1/_8$ teaspoon cinnamon
$1/_4$ teaspoon vanilla extract
$1/_4$ teaspoon rum – if it's for grown ups
Butter for the skillet
3 slices day-old Crusty Peasant or French bread per person

✳ Combine all of the ingredients except the butter and bread. Mix well.
✳ Heat the butter on a griddle or skillet over medium heat.
✳ While the pan is heating, soak the bread slices in the batter (be sure both sides are coated) and immediately place the slices on the heated skillet.
✳ Cook until golden brown on the bottom, flip the bread, and continue to cook until the other side is brown.
✳ Set the toast aside on a plate in a warm oven and continue cooking until all the bread is gone.

Variations:
I often make a special French Toast with cream cheese and jam in the center of two slices of bread. Here are my favorite combinations

Cranberry Bread
Marmalade
Cream cheese

Pumpkin bread
Cream cheese

French bread
Raspberry jam
Cream cheese

Frittata

2 tablespoons olive oil
1 medium zucchini, thinly sliced
8 medium mushrooms, thinly sliced
1 medium green pepper, seeded and thinly sliced
2 garlic cloves, minced
1 tablespoon basil, minced
1 tablespoon thyme, minced
$1/_2$ teaspoon Dijon mustard
8 eggs
$1/_2$ cup grated Parmesan
1 tablespoon olive oil

✳ Preheat oven to 350°. Heat a cast-iron skillet over medium heat and add the olive oil.
✳ Cook the veggies and garlic until soft.
✳ Whisk the rest of the ingredients in a bowl and pour the mixture over the veggies.
✳ Bake until the frittata has puffed up, around 30 to 40 minutes.

Fruit Compote

Makes approximately 4 cups

Makes approximately 4 cups

This is great on top of oatmeal, which is how we serve it on the boat. In the winter, my daughters Ella and Chlöe like it warmed up for breakfast with a little yogurt or milk in it. Below is my favorite combination of fruits, but I've also used currants, dried cranberries and dried blueberries. I would use these on special occasions. You can use a little rum or Grand Marnier in place of $^1/_4$ cup of the apple juice. And it tastes even better the next day!

1 cup dried apricots, whole or chopped
1 cup raisins
1 cup prunes, whole or chopped
1 apple, cored, peeled, and diced
$^1/_4$ cup brown sugar
$^3/_4$ teaspoon cinnamon
2 cups apple juice

✳ Put all the ingredients into a medium saucepan. Bring to a boil over medium-high heat; reduce heat to low, cover, and simmer until fruit is all cooked together, around 30 to 40 minutes.

✳ Serve warm or cold.

German Apple Pancake

This is one big pancake. My kids love to have this anytime of the day or night. In the winter we even have it for dinner, with cheddar cheese and a green salad with raisins, nuts and pears.

$^1/_2$ cup unbleached all-purpose flour
1 tablespoon sugar
$^1/_2$ teaspoon salt
2 large eggs
$^2/_3$ cup half and half
1 teaspoon vanilla extract
2 tablespoons unsalted butter
$1^1/_4$ pounds Granny Smith or Braeburn apples, peeled, quartered, cored
$^1/_4$ cup packed brown sugar
$^1/_4$ teaspoon ground cinnamon
1 teaspoon lemon juice
Confectioner's sugar for dusting

✳ Preheat oven to 500°. Adjust your oven rack to a middle/upper position.

✳ Whisk the flour, white sugar, and salt together in medium bowl.

✳ In a separate bowl, whisk the eggs, half and half, and vanilla.

✳ Whisk the wet and dry ingredients together until no lumps remain (about 20 seconds). Set the batter aside.

✳ Heat the butter in a 10-inch ovenproof, non-stick skillet over medium-high heat until sizzling.

✳ Add the apples, brown sugar and cinnamon and cook, stirring frequently with a heatproof rubber spatula, until the apples are golden brown (about 10 minutes).

✳ Remove from heat and stir in the lemon juice.

✳ Working quickly, pour the batter into the skillet around and over the apples. Place the skillet in the oven and immediately reduce heat to 425°. Bake until the pancake edges are brown and puffy, and have risen above edges of skillet (about 18 minutes).

✳ Using oven mitts remove the skillet from the oven. Loosen the edges of the pancake with a heatproof rubber spatula. REMEMBER THE SKILLET HANDLE IS BURNING HOT. Don't touch it without the oven mitts.

✳ Transfer the pancake onto a serving platter, dust with confectioner's sugar, cut into wedges, and serve.

Sour Cream Coffee Cake

From *A Taste of the Taber* Cookbook

Cake:

$^3/_4$ cup shortening
$^3/_4$ cup sugar
2 cups all-purpose flour
$^1/_2$ teaspoon salt
1 teaspoon baking powder
1 teaspoon baking soda
$^1/_2$ cup yogurt
$^1/_2$ cup sour cream
2 large eggs, beaten
1 teaspoon vanilla extract

Topping:

$^1/_2$ cup chopped walnuts
$^1/_2$ cup sugar
2 teaspoons ground cinnamon

* Preheat oven to 350°. Grease a 9 x 9-inch baking pan.
* In a large bowl, cream together the shortening and sugar.
* Mix in the flour, salt, baking powder and baking soda.
* Stir in the yogurt, sour cream, eggs and vanilla.
* In a separate bowl, mix together the topping ingredients.
* Pour the batter into the pan and sprinkle with the topping.
* Bake for 40-45 minutes, until a fork inserted in the center comes out clean.
* Cool in the pan and cut into squares.

Sticky Buns

Dough:

1 tablespoon yeast
$1^1/_2$ teaspoons salt
$^1/_4$ cup sugar
4 cups flour
1 cup warm water
$^1/_4$ cup vegetable oil
2 eggs, beaten

Filling:

4 tablespoons ($^1/_2$ stick) melted butter
$^3/_4$ cup packed brown sugar
$^1/_2$ cup currants
1 teaspoon cinnamon

Glaze:

$1^1/_2$ cups powdered sugar
1 to $1^1/_2$ tablespoons milk
1 teaspoon vanilla extract

* Combine all of the dry ingredients for the dough and mix briefly.
* Add the wet ingredients and add a bit more water if needed.
* Knead the dough for 10-15 minutes; cover and set aside to rise until doubled (about 1 hour).
* Punch down the dough and roll it out into a large rectangle $^1/_4$ to $^1/_2$-inch thick.
* Preheat oven to 350°. Grease a 9 x 13-inch pan.
* Brush the butter onto the dough and sprinkle the rest of the filling ingredients evenly over the dough.
* Gently roll and tuck the dough lengthwise until it is shaped like a log: cut it into 12 equal pieces.
* Place the rolls into the pan (so the spiral of filling faces up); cover and let rise until doubled.
* Bake until golden, about 30 minutes.
* Cool for five minutes.
* Whisk together the glaze ingredients, remove the buns from the pan, and drizzle them with the glaze.

Sue's Breakfast Muffins

Muffins:

$^1/_3$ cup shortening
$^1/_2$ cup sugar
1 large egg
$1^1/_2$ cups all-purpose flour
$1^1/_2$ teaspoons baking powder
$^1/_2$ teaspoon salt
$^1/_4$ teaspoon ground nutmeg
$^1/_2$ cup milk

Topping:

$^1/_2$ cup sugar
1 teaspoon ground cinnamon
6 tablespoons warm, melted butter

※ Preheat oven to 350°. Grease or paper muffin pans.

※ In a medium bowl, cream together the shortening and sugar; add the egg and mix well.

※ Sift the flour, baking powder, salt, and nutmeg into a separate bowl.

※ Mix one-third of the flour into the shortening mixture then one-third of the milk. Repeat 2 times.

※ Fill the muffin cups two-thirds full.

※ Bake for 20-25 minutes, until the muffins spring back when lightly pressed in the center.

※ Mix the sugar and cinnamon together. When the muffins are done, dip each muffin in the melted butter and immediately roll it in the cinnamon-sugar mixture.

Three-Grain Pancakes

$^3/_4$ cup all-purpose flour
$^1/_2$ cup whole wheat flour
$^1/_2$ cup rye flour
$^1/_4$ cup cornmeal
$1^1/_2$ tablespoons sugar
1 tablespoon baking powder
1 teaspoon salt
$^1/_4$ teaspoon baking soda
$1^1/_4$ to $1^1/_2$ cups milk
3 large eggs
3 tablespoons butter
Additional butter for cooking

* In a small pan or the microwave, melt the butter and set aside to cool slightly.
* Combine the dry ingredients in a large bowl.
* Make a well in the flour mixture. Stir in the milk and eggs; while mixing add the melted butter. Do not overmix.
* Let the mixture stand for 20-30 minutes.
* Heat a griddle or skillet over medium heat until hot, then add 1 tablespoon of butter. Pour or ladle the batter into the pan; when the pancakes start to set and you see bubbles popping on the pancakes, flip them and cook until the other side is brown.
* Place the pancakes in a warm oven until you've finished cooking.

When I have extra time in the early morning, I'll make the oatmeal this way. This calls for steel cut oats, but I make it with the old fashioned oats and it's just as delicious. The aroma of the toasting is really cozy.

3 cups water
1 cup whole milk
$\frac{1}{4}$ teaspoon salt
1 tablespoon unsalted butter
1 cup steel cut oats

✳ Bring the water, milk, and salt to a simmer in a large saucepan over medium heat.
✳ Meanwhile, heat the butter in a medium skillet over medium heat until it just begins to foam; add the oats and toast, stirring constantly, with a wooden spoon, until golden and fragrant, about $1\frac{1}{2}$ to 2 minutes.
✳ Stir the toasted oats into the simmering liquid; reduce heat to medium-low; simmer gently, uncovered, stirring occasionally, until the mixture thickens, about 40 minutes (20 minutes for old-fashioned oats).
✳ Remove from heat and let the oatmeal stand, uncovered, for 5 minutes before serving.

Appetizers

After an exhilarating day of sailing, our faces smiling and sunburned, the crew and passengers furl the huge canvas sails, clear the deck and enjoy a time of rest. The backdrop to this time of day may be granite rocks covered in seaweed, a curious seal popping up to see what's what, or soaring osprey searching for their dinners as the sun sinks on the horizon.

The appetizers that I serve on the boat all have to be easy and quick. Coming into an anchorage hard on the wind doesn't lend itself to fussy and time-consuming dishes. I dress these simple treats up with colorful herbs and flowers. When I make the Artichoke and Red Pepper Dip, it never gets a chance to cool; like pirates falling on a treasure, our passengers happily dip in. If we are lucky enough to have leftover lobster from the lobsterbake, I'll serve the Lobster Dip on Friday night as a special indulgence.

Crostini

Crostini are essentially slices of French bread drizzled with olive oil and toasted. They're easy to make and really dress up any appetizers. I'll often make an extra loaf of bread so that I can make Crostini to serve with appetizers. To make Crostini, slice a loaf of French bread into diagonal ¼-inch slices. Place them on a cookie pan and drizzle with olive oil. Bake at 350° until golden brown, turning once (about 15 minutes).

Artichoke and Red Pepper Dip   *Makes 3 cups*

This can be made ahead of time and stored in the fridge or freezer until you're ready to bake it.

1 8-ounce jar marinated artichokes, liquid drained, minced
1 small can chopped green chilies
1 small can chopped red peppers
$^1/_2$ cup mayonnaise
$^1/_2$ cup salsa
Fresh black pepper to taste
2 cups grated cheddar or Monterey Jack cheese

✳ Preheat oven to 400°.
✳ Mix all of the ingredients together then spoon the mixture into a large ovenproof platter or shallow casserole dish.
✳ Bake until bubbly and lightly brown on top, approximately 15 minutes.
✳ Serve with crackers or corn chips.

Green Olive Tapenade   *Makes 1 cup*

You can make the tapenade up to two weeks in advance. It gets better with time. This dip is great with goat cheese and spread on Crostini or crackers.

1 cup pitted green olives
2 tablespoons capers
2 anchovy fillets
$^1/_2$ cup packed fresh Italian parsley
2 cloves garlic
$^1/_4$ cup extra-virgin olive oil
Fresh black pepper to taste

✳ Because the olives and capers are so salty you may want to soak them in fresh water for a few minutes to release some of the salt. Drain them after soaking.
✳ Puree all the ingredients in a food processor.
✳ Refrigerate until ready to serve. Serve with Crostini.

Herbed Feta Cheese

This recipe is only practical if you have your own herb garden or can scam herbs from a friend's garden. Otherwise it gets to be pretty costly.

Marinade:

1 pound piece (or several large chunks) good quality feta cheese
8-10 fresh sage leaves
1 small handful fresh dill sprigs
5 sprigs fresh thyme
1 small bunch Greek oregano
4 sprigs of Italian parsley
1 teaspoon whole black peppercorns
$^1/_2$ teaspoon crushed red pepper
1 lemon, thinly sliced
Extra-virgin olive oil as needed

To Serve:

2 to 3 ripe tomatoes, sliced
1 lemon, thinly sliced
Sprigs of herbs for garnish

Marinade:

* Place the cheese, herbs, spices, and lemon slices in a Ziploc bag.
* Add olive oil until the cheese is covered (you'll use less oil if you squeeze out air as you add oil).
* Seal the bag and refrigerate at least 6 hours (24 hours is even better).

To Serve:

* Remove the cheese from the bag, reserving the oil.
* Cut the cheese into bite-size slices and arrange the slices on a platter with the sliced lemon and tomatoes.
* Drizzle with the reserved oil and garnish with herbs.
* Serve at room temperature with crackers or pita bread.

Guush
The games that the girls play on the boat are often inventive and use what we have on hand, rather than involving a lot of toys. The old adage – the kids want to play with the box more than the toy – is true. Guush is an idea a friend gave us – the girls love it. What's really fun about it is that the mixture will feel like a solid one minute and a liquid the next. Try it and see if you don't want to play with it too!
¾ cup cornstarch
6 tablespoons water
2-3 drops food coloring (optional)

Mix 'em all up in a bowl and play!

Ducktrap Smoked Mackerel Dip   *Serves 4-6*

Ducktrap is a local company – they make wonderful smoked fish. It's perfect for this recipe. It's also a great way to use up leftover salmon (see Variations).

4 ounces Ducktrap smoked mackerel
4 ounces softened cream cheese
1 tablespoon grated onion
$^1/_2$ teaspoon freshly ground black pepper
1 tablespoon diced chives
2 tablespoons lemon juice

✳ Combine all ingredients by hand or in a food processor.
✳ Refrigerate or serve immediately with French bread or crackers.

Variations
Replace the smoked mackerel with Ducktrap smoked trout or 1 cup cooked salmon.
Replace the chives with 1 tablespoon minced dill.
Replace lemon juice with lime juice.
Add horseradish.

Lobster Dip   *Serves 4-6*

The idea of having leftover lobster will seem absurd to most everyone who doesn't live in Maine, I know. However, after our weekly lobster bakes we often find we are able to treat ourselves to lobster a second time. This one is so simple.

1 cup coarsely chopped lobster meat (one 1-pound lobster)
$^1/_4$ cup (more, to taste) of Hellmann's mayonnaise
Worcestershire sauce to taste
Fresh ground black pepper to taste

✳ Mix it all together and taste for flavor.
✳ Serve with crackers.

Raspberry Fruit Dip

1 8-ounce package cream cheese
$^1/_2$ cup fresh or frozen raspberries
$^1/_4$ cup sugar
1 teaspoon lemon juice

✳ Mix all the ingredients in a food processor.
✳ Taste for flavor and serve with apples, pears, grapes and/or bananas.

Roasted garlic is about
as versatile as it gets.
Whenever we have
"Pasta Night" on board I
serve it so that folks
can spread it on their
bread, mush it into
their sauce or plunk a
few into their salad. I
also use it in egg
dishes, soups, stews
and dressings.

4 whole heads garlic
2 tablespoons olive oil

Preheat oven to 425°.
Slice the top off the
garlic heads and rub
away any loose skin.
Drizzle with olive oil and
roast until tender and
golden brown on top
(around 1 hour).

Sun-Dried Tomato Spread   *Makes approximately 2 cups*

1 cup sun-dried tomatoes packed in oil (not the kind you have to reconstitute), drained
$1/_4$ cup packed fresh Italian parsley
$1/_4$ cup packed fresh basil
$1/_2$ cup walnuts
$1/_2$ cup grated fresh Romano cheese
$1/_2$ head roasted garlic
Fresh pepper
Extra-virgin olive oil

* Combine all of the ingredients except the olive oil in a food processor and pulse them until they are completely mixed.
* Turn on the processor and add the olive oil in a steady stream just until the mixture gets loose enough to roll and turn over (rather than being bound up).
* Refrigerate at least 1 hour before serving. Overnight is even better.
* Serve with Crostini (page 50).

Warm Cheddar and Horseradish Dip   *Serves 4-6*

A more festive way to serve this dip is to dig out the center of a round loaf of bread and cut the center into 1-inch cubes. Warm the dip in a double boiler and pour it into the center of the bread and serve with the bread cubes.

4 ounces softened cream cheese
1 tablespoon grated onion
$1/_4$ teaspoon freshly ground black pepper
2 tablespoons horseradish
1 tablespoon lemon juice
1 tablespoon minced fresh parsley
$1/_2$ cup grated cheddar cheese

* Preheat oven to 375°.
* Combine all the ingredients by hand or in a food processor.
* Spoon the mixture onto an ovenproof platter.
* Bake for 20 minutes until the dip is bubbling around the edges.

From the Garden – Salads and Dressings

When we bought our house, the realtor said it needed a little TLC. This is realtor speak for "You'll need to gut the place." Our gardens and lawn were in the same shape – a few shoes and engine parts sticking up between patches of grass, but no flowers or herbs unless you count the comfrey taking charge in the back yard. It's been an ongoing project, but gradually, each year, I add more tilled area so that now we have over 1,000 square feet of garden from which I bring all of the herbs and flowers we use on the boat. Growing my own herbs means I can use them with an abandon I never would if I actually paid for them at the grocery store. Hence I've used nasturtium and pansy flowers in green salads, chive blossoms in the Warm Cheddar and Horseradish dip and lavender flowers and lemon thyme in Baking Powder Biscuits or to rub on a pork loin.

Most of the vegetables we serve onboard come from Agricola Farms, the local Community Supported Farm, to which we belong. These recipes are some of my favorites and they change according to what is in season. The roasted beet salad with goat cheese is a good example. Because we get such high quality produce from Agricola Farms, sometimes the simplest flavors are the best. While I love big, bold flavors, I'll sometimes just steam green beans that were picked that morning. Sautéed greens are another example of allowing the brightness of the vegetable to shine.

Salads

The best way to insure that your vegetables and fruits have flavor is to grow your own. Unfortunately not everyone has the time or inclination to garden, but we can still make sure our tables are full of fresh, good-tasting produce by buying locally. What is grown locally isn't grown to travel well, but to taste good; it's as fresh as possible and full of nutrients. Community Supported Agriculture or CSA is a wonderful way to support local farmers and to participate in the bounty of the land. Community Supported Farms can be found all over the country. With the purchase of a lump sum "share" in the farm each spring, "shareholders" receive baskets of the freshest local produce all summer long.

Banana Salsa

It's really important to make this salsa just before you serve it. It will sit for maybe half an hour, but is better if served immediately. It's also important to finely dice the peppers and onions because they don't have time to marinate.

        2 bananas (firm, but ripe), diced
        2 tablespoons finely diced red onion
        1 tablespoon each finely diced red and green pepper
        $^1/_2$ teaspoon freshly grated ginger
        1 teaspoon honey
        1 tablespoon extra-virgin olive oil
        Juice of one lime
        Salt and fresh black pepper to taste; use sparingly

* Gently toss all ingredients together; season with salt and pepper.

* Serve on top of the freshly grilled meat or seafood of your choice. It's great with grilled salmon, tuna, pork, or chicken.

Garbanzo Bean and Roasted Eggplant Salad *Serves 4-6*

        1 eggplant
        Juice of 1 lemon
        2 tablespoons balsamic vinegar
        4 tablespoons extra-virgin olive oil
        $^1/_2$ teaspoon salt
        Freshly ground black pepper to taste
        $^1/_2$ bunch minced parsley
        2 fresh tomatoes, diced
        2 16-ounce cans garbanzo beans, drained

* Preheat oven to 400°.

* Pierce the skin of the eggplant several times with a fork. Place the whole eggplant in a baking dish and roast it for 20 to 30 minutes (until you can squeeze it and it's soft). Cool the eggplant, scoop it out of the skin, and cut it into $^1/_2$-inch cubes.

* Whisk together the lemon juice, vinegar, olive oil, salt, and pepper and gently toss the mixture with the eggplant and remaining ingredients and serve.

Black Bean and Corn Salad

This salad is best if you can grill the corn, though you can use steamed or boiled corn in a pinch. I sometimes roast the corn when we are on a lobsterbake – just stick them on a roasting fork and turn them over the fire. You can also use it as a summer salsa for grilled chicken or fish.

4 ears of husked corn
1 tablespoon olive oil
1 15-ounce can black beans, drained and rinsed
$^1/_2$ jalapeno pepper, seeded and minced
1 red pepper, seeded and diced
$^1/_2$ cup loosely packed, fresh, chopped cilantro
$^1/_4$ cup diced red onion
Small clove garlic, minced
1 tablespoon extra-virgin olive oil
$^1/_2$ teaspoon salt
$^1/_4$ teaspoon freshly ground black pepper

❋ Brush the ears of corn with olive oil and place the ears directly on a hot grill. Cook until brown and tender, turning often, about 10 minutes.
❋ Cool slightly and use a sharp knife to cut the kernels off the cob.
❋ Toss the corn with the remaining ingredients and serve.

Chicken, Roasted Red Pepper and Couscous Salad

Serves 6-8

3 cups water
1 teaspoon salt
2 pounds boneless skinless chicken breasts
2 cups couscous
1 large red pepper, roasted, seeded, and diced
$^1/_4$ cup minced chives
3 slices cooked bacon, crumbled

Vinaigrette:

$^1/_4$ cup extra-virgin olive oil
1 tablespoon Dijon mustard
2 tablespoons soy sauce
Several grinds on the pepper mill
2 tablespoons white wine vinegar

* Bring the water and salt to a boil. Add the chicken and reduce the heat until the liquid is just below a simmer and cook for 20 minutes.
* Reserve 2 cups of the liquid, remove the chicken from the rest of the liquid, and set the chicken aside to cool.
* Bring the reserved liquid to a boil and remove from heat. Stir in the couscous, cover, and let it sit for 5 minutes.
* Dice the cooled chicken.
* Whisk together the vinaigrette ingredients.
* Fluff the couscous with a fork; toss it with the vinaigrette, chicken, and remaining ingredients.

Extra-Virgin or Virgin Olive Oil?

When you heat extra-virgin olive oil, the wonderful flavors dissipate, so it makes more sense to use virgin olive oil or even pure olive oil instead of extra-virgin for cooking. However, extra-virgin olive oil does make a big taste difference when you're not going to heat it. Use it when you are making salads, salsas or sauces that won't be heated.

Couscous and Chickpea Salad Serves 6-8

$1^1/_4$ cups water
$^1/_2$ teaspoon salt
1 cup uncooked couscous
3 tablespoons white wine vinegar
1 garlic clove, minced
1 tablespoon Dijon mustard
$^1/_4$ teaspoon sugar
$^1/_3$ cup extra-virgin olive oil
1 15-ounce can chickpeas, drained
2 small red bell peppers, seeded and diced
4 scallions, minced
1 large carrot, diced
$^1/_2$ cup pitted and diced Kalamata olives
$^3/_4$ cup chopped fresh mint (save a few sprigs for garnish)
6 ounces crumbled feta cheese

✳ Bring the water and salt to a boil.
✳ Add the couscous, stir briefly, cover, and remove from heat. Let it sit 5 minutes.
✳ While the couscous is sitting whisk together the vinegar, garlic, mustard, sugar, and olive oil.
✳ Fluff the couscous then toss it with the in the chickpeas, peppers, scallions, carrots, olives, and vinegar mixture.
✳ Add the feta cheese, chill, and serve.

Lentil and Sun-Dried Tomato Salad

Serves 6-8

I like French lentils for this recipe as they are tastier and they don't get mushy as fast.

2 cups lentils
$^1/_2$ cup sun-dried tomatoes
1 medium onion, finely chopped
1 tablespoon minced fresh oregano
$1^1/_2$ cups peeled and diced cucumber
2 tablespoons olive oil
$^1/_4$ teaspoon each salt and freshly ground black pepper
4 tablespoons balsamic vinegar
Juice of one lemon
Goat or feta cheese for garnish (optional)

✳ Cook the lentils in salted, boiling water until done, about 25 minutes.

✳ Drain and rinse with cold water.

✳ Combine the lentils with the remaining ingredients (except the cheese).

✳ Garnish with crumbled cheese and serve.

Melon and Israeli Couscous Salad   *Serves 6-8*

This salad was inspired by a local restaurant called Market on Main (M.O.M.). It seemed like an odd combination, but I'm always trying the interesting dishes on menus. The tart fruits – grapes and citrus – really give this dish the punch that makes it great. I can find Israeli couscous at our local health food store and at the grocery store in the specialty foods section.

2 cups Israeli couscous
1 cup diced watermelon
1 cup diced honeydew
1 cup diced cantaloupe
1 cup green grapes, cut in half
1 cup currants
$^1/_4$ cup vegetable oil
Juice and zest of 1 lemon
Juice and zest of 1 orange
Juice of 1 lime
1 teaspoon honey
1 tablespoon minced fresh mint
Pinch of salt
Mint leaves and lemon wedges for garnish

* Cook the couscous according to the package directions.
* Drain and rinse with cold water; set aside.
* While the couscous is cooking, mix the remaining ingredients together in a large bowl.
* Toss the drained couscous into the fruit, garnish with mint leaves and citrus wedges and serve.

Roasted Beet and Goat Cheese Salad   *Serves 8*

We get the most wonderful beets from Agricola Farms. Obviously the fresher the beets, the better the salad. I adapt this recipe to what's available; it's really flexible. I replace the roasted beets with roasted onions, roasted squash or steamed beans. The pecans become pine nuts or walnuts. The goat cheese becomes a feta or a bleu cheese; sometimes I add lemon juice to the dressing.

> 1 cup whole pecans
> 2 pounds fresh beets, stemmed and scrubbed
> 2 tablespoons olive oil
> $^1/_4$ teaspoon salt
> $^1/_4$ teaspoon fresh ground black pepper
> 8 ounces fresh goat cheese
> 1 head romaine lettuce, washed, in bite-size pieces
> 2 tablespoons olive oil
> 2 tablespoons balsamic vinegar
> Salt and pepper

✳ Preheat oven to 450°.

✳ Place the pecans in a pie pan and toast in the oven for 7 minutes.

✳ Cut the beets in quarters or eighths, depending on how big they are.

✳ Toss the beets with the oil, salt, and pepper in a roasting pan.

✳ Roast until the beets are tender when pierced with a fork, about 45 minutes to an hour. Set the beets aside to cool slightly, and be sure to reserve any excess liquid in the roasting pan.

✳ Toss half of the pecans and half of the goat cheese with the lettuce, beets, oil, vinegar and salt and pepper.

✳ Sprinkle the reserved beet liquid on top of the salad with the rest of the pecans and goat cheese and serve.

There are times when there is nothing better than sautéed greens with little or no embellishment. Other times I'll boost the flavor with Parmesan or feta cheese, roasted nuts, and/or diced tomatoes.

1 pound greens (spinach, Swiss chard, or dandelion greens are all good)
2 tablespoons olive oil
1 large clove garlic, minced
2 teaspoons soy sauce
2 teaspoons balsamic vinegar
Freshly ground black pepper

* Wash then roughly chop the greens.
* Heat a large skillet over medium-high heat.
* Add the olive oil and garlic; cook the garlic for 30 seconds.
* Add the greens, tossing gently, then add the rest of the ingredients and toss again. Cook until the greens are tender. Cooking times will vary depending on the green. Spinach will go the fastest.

A Variation from Agricola Farms:
1 pound greens (spinach, Swiss chard, or dandelion greens are all good)
2 tablespoons olive oil
$1/_4$ teaspoon salt
1 tablespoon lemon juice
Red pepper flakes (optional)

Follow instructions above.

Salad Dressings

Creamy Blue Cheese Dressing

Makes 1 cup

This can be refrigerated for several days – it only gets better.

2$^{1}/_{2}$ ounces blue cheese, crumbled
5 tablespoons buttermilk
3 tablespoons sour cream
2 tablespoons mayonnaise
2 teaspoons white wine vinegar
$^{1}/_{4}$ teaspoon sugar
1 clove garlic, minced
$^{1}/_{8}$ teaspoon salt
$^{1}/_{8}$ teaspoon fresh pepper
Dash of Worcestershire

✳ Whisk all the ingredients together.
✳ Refrigerate.

Dana's Maple-Dill Dressing

Makes 2 cups

3 tablespoons fresh lemon juice
2 tablespoons red wine vinegar
$^{1}/_{2}$ cup maple syrup
1 bunch fresh dill or 1$^{1}/_{2}$ tablespoons dry dill
4$^{1}/_{2}$ teaspoons soy sauce
1 cup toasted almonds, hazelnuts, or pine nuts
4 garlic cloves, roughly chopped
$^{1}/_{4}$ teaspoon grated lemon rind
1$^{1}/_{3}$ cups olive oil

✳ Puree everything except the oil in a food processor or blender.
✳ With the blender running gradually pour in the olive oil (doesn't have to be too slow – just don't pour it in all at once).
✳ This can be made well in advance and refrigerated.

Lemon Parmesan Dressing

  Extra virgin olive oil
  Juice from 1 lemon
  Grated or shaved fresh parmesan cheese to taste
  Salt and freshly ground black pepper to taste

✳ Toss greens with olive oil and then the rest of the ingredients to your liking.

Mom's Blue Cheese Vinaigrette   *Makes about 1 cup*

This dressing will hold in the refrigerator for two weeks.

  $^1/_4$ cup red wine vinegar
  3 to 4 ounces blue cheese, crumbled
  3 scallions, thinly sliced
  $^1/_4$ teaspoon salt
  $^1/_4$ teaspoon paprika
  $^1/_8$ teaspoon dry mustard
  $^1/_8$ teaspoon black pepper
  $^3/_4$ cup salad oil

✳ Pulse all the ingredients except the oil in a food processor.
✳ With the food processor running, gradually add the oil (this doesn't need to be slow, just don't dump it in all at once).

Creamy Herb Dressing

$1/4$ bunch dill leaves
$1/4$ bunch flat-leaf parsley
$1/4$ bunch thyme
$1/2$ bunch chives
$3/4$ cup mayonnaise
$1/2$ cup buttermilk
2 tablespoons cider vinegar
$1/2$ teaspoon coarse salt
$1/8$ teaspoon freshly ground black pepper
$3/4$ teaspoon hot sauce

❋ Combine the dill, parsley, thyme, and chives with the mayonnaise in a food processor until the herbs are finely chopped.
❋ While the processor is running, slowly pour in the buttermilk.
❋ Add the vinegar, salt, pepper and hot sauce.
❋ Taste and adjust seasoning.
❋ Pour into a bottle or jar and refrigerate for up to 2 weeks.

Soups

When the breezes turn brisk or the fog rolls in, there's nothing more soothing than wrapping your hands around a bowl of warm, comforting soup. We serve lunch on deck every day (unless we've a bit of inclement weather) – often soups or stews (stews are in the Main Course section). The Tomato Soup with Herbed Yogurt goes really well with Mom's Brown Bread; Golden Northern Corn Bread is the perfect combination with the Black Bean Chili or Black Bean and Jasmine Rice Soup.

Baby Soup
When Chlöe was two, she liked to sit in the galley and help with dishes. As anyone who has experienced a two-year-old close to water knows, "help" is the last thing you need if you care about being done with dishes in this century. "Baby Soup" was what we played instead. She'd sit in the big stew pot and we'd "season" her with salt, pepper and spices and stir with the long wooden spoon (of course, this was always the last pot washed). Later this turned into a deck game where we'd give both girls (Ella, now 3 and Chlöe, 6) Dixie cups of spices and herbs, some kitchen utensils and a deck bucket of salt water.

Bermuda Fish Chowder

This stew is really enhanced by the addition of two condiments: dark rum and spiced sherry. To make spiced sherry, fill a small jar or cruet with sherry and stuff a whole jalapeno pepper into it. Let it sit for at least a day. The spiced sherry will keep for months.

1 tablespoon olive oil
2 large onions, diced
4 large carrots, diced
3 stalks celery, diced
1 large green pepper, seeded and diced
1 jalapeno pepper, seeded and diced
4 medium-sized potatoes, diced
6 cloves garlic, minced
1 teaspoon salt
6 ounces tomato paste
$1^1/_2$ teaspoons allspice
$^1/_2$ teaspoon ground cloves
$^1/_2$ teaspoon cayenne pepper
3 bay leaves
1 28-ounce can diced tomatoes
6 cups water or fish stock
1 teaspoon Tabasco sauce
1 teaspoon Worcestershire sauce
1 tablespoon lemon juice
2 pounds of haddock or other white fish

✳ Heat the olive oil in a medium-sized stockpot over medium-high heat. Add the olive oil, onions, carrots, celery and peppers to the pot and sauté until the vegetables are golden brown.
✳ Add the potatoes, garlic, salt, tomato paste and spices and cook for another 5 to 10 minutes.
✳ Add the rest of the ingredients except for the fish.
✳ Simmer, uncovered, for 1 hour.
✳ Fifteen minutes before serving add the fish and stir gently. Stir again before serving to break up the fish.
✳ Serve with the spiced sherry and rum.

Black Bean Chili

We serve this on the boat with all the fixin's: grated cheddar cheese, chopped onions, sour cream, Pico de Gallo (next page), corn bread and corn chips. We always serve it with a salad too and on hot days everyone will make a taco salad.

2 tablespoons olive oil
1 pound ground beef
1 teaspoon salt
2 large onions, chopped
1 large green pepper, seeded and diced
9 cloves garlic, minced
2 tablespoons cumin
2 tablespoons chili powder
6 cups beef stock
1 28-ounce can diced tomatoes
2 cups dried black beans, or 2 16-ounce cans cooked black beans
1 teaspoon salt
$^1/_2$ teaspoon pepper

✷ Heat a stockpot over medium heat.

✷ Add the oil, ground beef and salt and cook until browned.

✷ Add the onions, pepper, garlic, cumin, and chili powder. Cook until the onions are translucent.

✷ Add the remaining ingredients; reduce heat and simmer, uncovered, for 1 hour.

Pico de Gallo

This is an easy salsa we make often to serve with either the Black Bean Chili or the Black Bean and Jasmine Rice Soup. It's great with both.

3 fresh tomatoes, seeded and diced
1 tablespoon minced cilantro
Juice of 1 lime
1 small onion, minced
1 clove garlic, minced
$^1/_2$ teaspoon salt
$^1/_4$ teaspoon freshly ground black pepper
2 tablespoons extra-virgin olive oil

✳ Combine all the ingredients in a bowl and serve. Makes 2-3 cups.

Black Bean and Jasmine Rice Soup   *Serves 4-6*

We often serve this soup with Pico de Gallo (previous page).

  2 tablespoons olive oil
  2 large onions, diced
  1 large green pepper, seeded and diced
  1 dried Ancho chili, reconstituted and minced
  9 cloves garlic, minced
  1 tablespoon cumin
  1 teaspoon salt
  1 14-ounce can diced tomatoes
  1 16-ounce can black beans
  5 cups chicken or vegetable stock
  Juice of 1 lime
  $^1/_2$ cup jasmine rice

Garnish:

  Sour cream
  Lime wedges
  Coarsely chopped cilantro

✳ Heat the olive oil in a medium-sized stockpot over medium-high heat; add the onions, peppers, garlic, cumin and salt to the pot and cook until the onions are translucent.

✳ Add the remaining ingredients except for the rice and simmer, uncovered, for 45 minutes.

✳ Add the jasmine rice and simmer for another 15 minutes. Add additional stock or water if needed.

✳ Garnish with sour cream, lime wedges, and cilantro.

There are three ingredients that make this a traditional chowder: salt pork, day old biscuits or saltines and milk. The more you substitute the less traditional your chowder will be. Notice that there is no butter or flour to thicken the chowder. If there were, then it would be Cream of Clam Soup, not chowder. This is a very versatile recipe. I've listed some of my favorite variations below.

$^1/_4$ pound salt pork, scored or 2 strips of bacon, diced
2 stalks celery, chopped
1 large onion, chopped
1 large or two small potatoes, diced
$^1/_2$ cup Saltines or oyster crackers, crumbled (it's even better if you have day old biscuits to crumble)
1 8-ounce bottle clam juice
2 10-ounce cans chopped clams (with liquid)
1 can evaporated milk
2 cups water
Fresh ground black pepper to taste

✳ Heat a medium-sized stockpot on medium-high heat. Place the scored salt pork in the pot. Render the pork for several minutes.
✳ Add the onions and celery to the pot and cook until translucent.
✳ Reduce heat to medium, add the potatoes and crackers, and cook for 3 to 5 minutes.
✳ Add the clam juice, evaporated milk, water, and fresh pepper.
✳ Reduce to low and cook, uncovered, for at least one hour.
✳ Add the canned clams and cook another 5 minutes before serving.

Variations
Whole Clam Chowder
Replace the canned clams with 1 pound of clams in the shell
Cornmeal

Before starting the chowder, place the clams in cold, salted water and sprinkle them with the cornmeal. Leave the clams to soak while you prepare the broth.
When the broth is ready, rinse the clams and add them to the pot cover, and turn off the heat when the clams open (about 5-10 minutes)
Serve immediately.

Salmon and Corn Chowder

Replace the clams with 1 pound of fresh, boneless salmon.
Cut the kernels off of two ears of corn.
Add the cobs when you add the clam juice and water;
simmer 1 hour.
Remove the cobs, add the salmon and the corn kernels,
cover, and cook another 10 minutes before serving. Stir
the salmon to break it into bite-size pieces before serving.

Haddock Chowder
Replace the clams with 1 pound of fresh, boneless had-
dock.
Add the haddock, cover, and cook another 10 minutes
before serving. Stir the haddock to break it into bite-size
pieces before serving.

Leek and Lobster Chowder
Replace 1 cup onions with 1 cup leeks.
Replace clams with 2 Maine lobsters.
Add the whole lobsters to the stock once it begins to
simmer and cover. Remove the lobsters as soon as their
shells are bright red.
Allow all of the juice in the lobsters to drain into the
stockpot; cool the lobsters in a bowl while the broth
continues to simmer, uncovered.
When they are cool, remove the meat from the shells and
pour the excess liquid back into the stockpot.
Cut the meat into $1/2$-inch pieces and add to the pot just
before serving.

On top of any of these fancier chowders you could serve
non-traditional garnishes such as chopped scallions,
chopped fresh herbs, crème fraiche (or sour cream), or
homemade croutons.

Chowder Secrets
A few tips for making the
most flavorful chowder:
Once the salt pork is
rendered it's very impor-
tant to give the onions
and the celery time to
become translucent. If a
little brown develops on
the bottom of the pan,
even better, just don't
burn it. Brown is good,
black is not! This is what
makes a flavorful soup.
The same is true when you
add the potatoes and the
biscuits or Saltines; let
the bottom of the pan
become a little brown
before you add the water
and the clam juice.
The reason that you add
evaporated milk rather
than fresh milk is that
fresh milk will curdle — not
so pretty or tasty.
It's important to wait to
add the clams (or any fish)
until the end. If you don't
you'll have rubber bands in
your chowder rather than
clams.

Sometimes I have leftover roasted garlic and I use it in place of the fresh garlic. If you have an herb garden like I do, then by all means use fresh herbs in place of the dried.

2 tablespoons olive oil
1 pound sweet Italian sausage, cut into -inch slices (or hot if you want a spicier soup)
2 large onions, diced
9 cloves garlic, minced
1 teaspoon salt
$^1/_2$ teaspoon fresh black pepper
2 teaspoons dried oregano
2 teaspoons dried marjoram
2 teaspoons dried thyme
2 teaspoons dried basil
1 zucchini, quartered and chopped
1 summer squash, quartered and chopped
2 potatoes, peeled and diced
1 cup red wine
1 14-ounce can diced tomatoes
4 to 5 cups chicken stock
$^1/_2$ cup cream (optional)
2 cups chopped spinach or kale

❋ Heat the olive oil in a medium-sized stockpot over medium-high heat.

❋ Add the sausage and sauté until brown.

❋ Add the onions, garlic, salt, pepper and herbs and continue to cook until the onions are translucent.

❋ Add the zucchini and summer squash and cook for another 5 minutes.

❋ Add the potatoes, wine, tomatoes, stock and optional cream; simmer for 45 minutes. Add more stock if needed. If you are using spinach, add it and cook another minute or two. If you are using kale, add it and cook for an additional 15 minutes.

Mushroom Barley Soup

3 tablespoons butter
2 cloves garlic, minced
1 large onion, chopped
1 pound sliced fresh mushrooms
$^1/_2$ cup pearled barley
6 cups chicken stock, vegetable stock, or water
$^1/_3$ cup tamari
$^1/_3$ cup dry sherry

✳ Melt the butter in a medium-sized stockpot over medium heat; add the onions and garlic and cook until the onions are translucent.

✳ Add the mushrooms and cook until tender.

✳ Add the remaining ingredients. Bring the soup to a boil; reduce heat and simmer, uncovered, for about 20 minutes, until the barley is completely cooked.

Spinach Gorgonzola Soup

$^1/_4$ cup ($^1/_2$ stick) butter
3 large onions, chopped
6 cloves garlic, minced
$^1/_2$ teaspoon salt
$^1/_4$ teaspoon freshly ground black pepper
2 teaspoons thyme
4 ounces Gorgonzola cheese
4 cups chicken or vegetable stock
5 ounces spinach, washed and julienned
2 cups peeled, seeded, and diced tomatoes

✳ Melt the butter in a stockpot over medium-high heat; add the onion, garlic, salt, pepper and thyme and cook until the onions are translucent.

✳ Add the Gorgonzola and chicken stock; bring the stock to a simmer then puree it in a blender or food processor.

✳ Place the spinach in the stockpot and cook for 1 minute. Add the tomatoes and pureed stock, simmer, and serve.

Thai Red Curry Soup

2 cups dry white wine
Bottom 4 inches of 3 fresh lemon grass stalks, thinly sliced
1 tablespoon matchstick size pieces peeled fresh ginger
2 cloves garlic, minced
4 cups bottled clam juice
4 cups canned, unsweetened coconut milk
2 teaspoons red curry paste
1 teaspoon grated lime peel
3 tablespoons corn starch
2 tablespoons water
$^1/_4$ cup thinly sliced fresh basil
1 tablespoon lemon juice
8 ounces snapper fillet, cut into $^1/_2$-inch cubes
16 medium uncooked shrimp, peeled, deveined, and halved

✳ Combine the wine, lemongrass, ginger, and garlic in a large, heavy-duty saucepan. Bring to a boil over medium-high heat.
✳ Add the clam juice and coconut milk and simmer about 15 minutes.
✳ Stir in the curry paste and lime peel.
✳ Mix the cornstarch and water in small bowl until smooth. Add to the soup and bring to a boil, stirring. Reduce heat and simmer 5 minutes, stirring occasionally.
✳ Add the basil, lemon juice, fish and shrimp; simmer just until the fish is cooked through, about 2 minutes. Season to taste and serve.

Tomato Soup with Herbed Yogurt

Serves 4-6

Soup:

1 tablespoon olive oil
1 large onion, sliced
3 cloves garlic, minced
Juice and zest of half an orange
1 tablespoon dried basil
1 tablespoon dried marjoram
1 tablespoon dried cumin
$^1/_4$ teaspoon red pepper flakes
2 28-ounce cans crushed tomatoes
$1^1/_2$ cups chicken or vegetable stock
1 square (1 ounce) bittersweet chocolate

Herbed Yogurt:

$^1/_2$ cup plain yogurt
1 green onion, diced
$1^1/_2$ tablespoons minced fresh basil
1 small clove garlic, minced

* Heat a stockpot over medium-high heat and add the olive oil, onion, garlic, orange zest, orange juice and spices.
* Cook until the onions are translucent.
* Add the rest of ingredients and simmer, uncovered, for 1 hour.
* Meanwhile whisk the yogurt ingredients together.
* Serve with a dollop of herbed yogurt.

Turnip and Leek Soup

I created this soup to deal with a mountain of turnips that we received from Agricola Farms. It reminds me of potato and leek soup – just a tasty twist on a classic.

2 tablespoons butter
1 large onion, chopped
3 cups cleaned and chopped leeks
6 cups peeled and coarsely chopped turnips
2 teaspoons salt
1 teaspoon freshly grated nutmeg
$1^1/_2$ tablespoons freshly grated ginger
1 cup white wine
2 cups vegetable stock
1 cup sour cream for garnish

✳ Melt the butter in a large stockpot over medium-high heat Add everything but the wine, stock, and sour cream and cook until the onions are translucent.

✳ Add the wine and stock and simmer for at least 30 minutes.

✳ For a more rustic soup, leave it as it is; to fancy it up a bit, whiz everything in the blender.

✳ Garnish with a dollop of sour cream.

Sides

Agricola Farms is a Community Supported Farm in Union, Maine run by husband and wife Mark Hedrich and Linda Rose. Community Supported Agriculture, or CSA, is a wonderful way to support local farming. Each family buys a share, paying one lump sum in the spring. Then all summer long we receive baskets of local produce. We buy four shares and the beautiful, mostly organic produce provided all summer long makes the food on the boat extra special. I can't wait to see what comes in the boxes every week. The special lettuces, greens and even a few tomatoes that arrive in June are so welcome after a year without them. By August we are overflowing with heirloom tomatoes, corn picked that morning and squashes of all different shapes and colors. Fall brings, of course, winter squashes, root vegetables and more lettuce. We get big pumpkins too and after the passengers and crew have carved their funniest or most gruesome face in them, we put them on deck with tea candles to light our way to the heads at night.

$^1/_4$ cup ($^1/_2$ stick) butter
2 stalks celery, chopped
1 large onion, chopped
2 cups barley
$^1/_2$ teaspoon salt
$^1/_2$ white wine
$3^1/_2$ cups chicken stock
Freshly ground black pepper to taste
$^1/_2$ cup grated Parmesan cheese

✳ Melt the butter in a medium saucepan over medium-high heat.
✳ Add the celery and onions and cook until translucent.
✳ Add the barley, salt, wine and 1 cup of chicken stock.
✳ Stir the mixture frequently over low heat, adding more stock as it is absorbed.
✳ When the barley is done, stir in the Parmesan and serve.

Cheesy Potatoes

My crew calls this recipe "cheesy potatoes," but it's really a classic potato gratin. I serve this with *Riggin* Ham and roasted onions.

> 2 pounds Yukon gold or russet potatoes, peeled
> 3 cups whipping or heavy cream
> 1 teaspoon coarse salt
> $^1/_8$ teaspoon freshly ground black pepper
> 1 generous pinch freshly grated nutmeg
> 2 whole cloves garlic
> $^3/_4$ cup finely shredded Gruyere, Emmenthaler, or Comte cheese

✳ Preheat the oven to 400°. Butter a 9 x 13-inch baking dish.

✳ Using a very sharp knife or mandolin, carefully cut the potatoes into 1/8-inch slices.

✳ Bring everything but the cheese to a boil in a large, heavy saucepan over medium-high heat. Stir occasionally and very gently so you don't break up the potato slices.

✳ When the cream boils, pour the mixture into the prepared baking dish; remove the garlic cloves and shake the dish to settle the potato slices.

✳ Sprinkle the cheese evenly over the potatoes.

✳ Bake until the top is deep golden brown, the cream has thickened, and the potatoes are extremely tender when pierced with a knife, about 40 minutes.

✳ Don't worry if the dish looks too liquid at this point; it will set up as it cools a bit. Before serving, let the potatoes cool until they're very warm but not hot (about 15 minutes).

Cinnamon Roasted Sweet Potatoes   *Serves 4-6*

3 tablespoons butter
1 teaspoon cinnamon
2 large sweet potatoes or three small, cut into a total of 6 pieces
$^1/_2$ teaspoon salt
$^1/_4$ teaspoon freshly ground black pepper

✳ Preheat oven to 375°.
✳ Melt the butter and the cinnamon.
✳ Place the potatoes in a baking pan and toss with the melted butter and cinnamon mixture.
✳ Sprinkle with salt and pepper and roast for 1 hour, until the potatoes are tender.

Garlic Mashed Potatoes   Serves 4

I've used olive oil in these potatoes as well. It's a great way to lower the fat content – or substitute if you find yourself in the middle of Penobscot Bay with very little butter left for the week (oops!).

4-6 Yukon Gold or russet potatoes, peeled and quartered
1 whole head of garlic, peeled
1 tablespoon salt (for the water)
$^1/_4$ cup ($^1/_2$ stick) butter
$^1/_2$ cup milk
$^3/_4$ teaspoon salt
Pinch of white pepper

✳ Place the potatoes, garlic and salt in a pot filled with cold water.
✳ Bring to a boil, reduce heat and simmer until the potatoes are tender when poked with a fork.
✳ Drain the water and add the remaining ingredients. Mash the potatoes either by hand or with a mixer. Add more milk if necessary.

Goat Cheese And Dill Mashed Potatoes *Serves 4 to 6*

This dish is really good with roast beef. You can make the potatoes ahead of time and reheat them in the microwave.

4 russet potatoes, peeled and cut into large pieces
6 ounces goat cheese
2 tablespoons butter
$1^1/_2$ teaspoons minced fresh dill
Salt and freshly ground white pepper to taste

✳ Place the potatoes in a saucepan, and cover them with cold, salted water. Bring the water to a boil over high heat; reduce heat and simmer until tender, approximately 20 minutes.
✳ Drain the potatoes and put them in a food processor with remaining ingredients.
✳ Pulse just until blended - no more or you will have wallpaper paste. If you don't have a food processor, just mash them with a potato masher or a hand mixer. However you make it, don't overmix.

Mom's Potato Casserole

This is one my mom used to make for brunches. It reminds me of when I was little. Now she uses it for all the brunch showers she holds for the grownup kids getting married and having babies.

1 large onion, coarsely chopped
1 tablespoon butter
1 can condensed Cream of Mushroom soup
8 ounces sharp cheddar cheese, grated
1 pound carton sour cream
2 pounds frozen hash browns
Freshly ground black pepper to taste

* Preheat oven to 350°.
* Cook the onions in the butter over medium heat until translucent.
* Mix the onions together with the remaining ingredients and spoon into a 9 x 13-inch ungreased pan.
* Bake until golden brown, about 40 minutes.

Polenta

1 cup medium-coarse or coarse cornmeal (preferably organic stoneground)
4 cups water, or 2 cups each water and milk
1 tablespoon butter or olive oil
1 teaspoon salt (to taste)

* Preheat the oven to 350°. Grease a 3 quart non-stick ovenproof skillet.
* Mix all the ingredients in the skillet and stir with a fork.
* Bake, uncovered, for 40 minutes (the mixture will separate and take more than half the cooking time to come together).
* Stir the polenta, taste, add salt if needed, and bake for another 10 minutes.
* Remove the skillet from the oven (remember that the WHOLE SKILLET IS HOT) and let the polenta rest in the pan for 5 minutes.
* (It's a good practice to throw a thick hand towel or oven mitt over the handle to minimize the chance of badly burning your hand if you forget.)
* Cut into wedges and serve.

Potato Gratin Serves 4-6

This recipe is from **The Essential Vegetarian Cookbook.**

> 2 teaspoons olive oil
> 2 cloves garlic, minced
> 1 medium onion, sliced thin
> 4-6 potatoes (preferably Yukon Gold), unpeeled, sliced thin
> $1/_2$ cup chicken or vegetable broth
> $1/_4$ cup minced parsley
> 3 tablespoons grated Parmesan or Romano cheese
> Salt and freshly grated black pepper to taste

* Heat the oil in a large skillet over medium-high heat; add the garlic and onions, reduce heat to medium-low, and cook, stirring frequently, until the onions have softened (about 6 minutes).
* Add the potatoes and broth.
* Cover and continue cooking until the potatoes are soft enough to mash with the back of a spoon, about 20 minutes.
* Add more broth if necessary to prevent sticking.
* Preheat the broiler.
* Lightly grease an 8-inch gratin dish or baking dish.
* Mash the potatoes coarsely with the back of a spoon or fork; stir in the parsley and spoon it into the prepared gratin dish, spreading evenly.
* Sprinkle the potato mixture with the grated cheese.
* Broil until the top is golden brown, about 3 minutes.

Potato Pancakes

1 small onion, peeled and grated
3 large Yukon gold potatoes, peeled and grated
$^1/_2$ teaspoon salt
$^1/_4$ teaspoon freshly ground black pepper
1 large egg white
3 tablespoons butter
Sour cream for garnish

* Place the onion in a strainer and press out as much moisture as possible.
* Combine all the remaining ingredients except the butter and sour cream.
* Heat a skillet on medium heat and add a tablespoon of butter.
* Drop a spoonful of the potato mixture onto the skillet and flatten gently with the back of the spoon.
* Brown on each side about 5 minutes each.
* Add more butter to the pan if needed.
* Serve with sour cream.

Potatoes Roasted with Red Wine   Serves 4-6

These are Jon's all-time favorite potatoes. I serve them with the roasted pork loin.

6 to 8 medium-sized red potatoes, cut into 1-inch pieces
$1^1/_2$ to 2 teaspoons salt
$^1/_2$ teaspoon fresh black pepper
1 whole head garlic, peeled
2 to 3 cups red wine
$^1/_2$ cup heavy cream

✻ Preheat oven to 375°.
✻ Put all the ingredients except the cream into a 9 x 13-inch baking dish. Cover and bake for 1 hour, stirring once or twice.
✻ Remove cover, add cream and bake uncovered for another 10 minutes.

Rosemary Potatoes

4-6 potatoes
3 sprigs of rosemary
4 to 6 tablespoons olive oil
$1^1/_2$ to 2 teaspoons salt
$^1/_2$ teaspoon fresh black pepper

✳ Preheat oven to 375°.
✳ Cut the potatoes into $^1/_4$-inch thick slices, being careful to not slice them through completely.
✳ Insert a few rosemary leaves between each slice.
✳ Toss with the olive oil, salt and pepper and place in an 8-inch baking pan.
✳ Bake, uncovered, until the potatoes are tender, approximately 1 hours.

Yorkshire Pudding

This is a classic that I often serve with Riggin Roast Beef.

1 cup all-purpose flour
$^1/_2$ teaspoon salt
$^1/_4$ teaspoon freshly ground black pepper
2 eggs
$1^1/_2$ to $1^3/_4$ cups milk
Drippings from roast beef (you can substitute olive oil or bacon fat)

✳ Preheat oven to 350°.
✳ Sift the dry ingredients into a bowl.
✳ Make a well in the center; stir in the eggs, then add the milk and stir, gradually incorporating the flour until you reach the sides of the bowl.
✳ Cover and refrigerate 30 minutes.
✳ Meanwhile, heat a 9-inch cast iron skillet or muffin tins in the oven until the pan (or muffin tins) are very hot. Add drippings to the pan and immediately pour in the batter.
✳ Bake uncovered, approximately 25-30 minutes. The pudding is done when it's puffy, golden brown and crispy.
✳ Serve immediately (or keep in a warm oven for up to 15 minutes).

Main Courses

Cooking on a Woodstove

When I'm down in the galley by my woodstove, folks will often say the stove reminds them of their grandmother. A woodstove is something most of our grandmothers or great-grandmothers used every day, but its use is becoming a lost art. We do our best to keep it alive on the Riggin.

Woodstoves are ideal for soups, stews and roasts because these dishes all lend themselves to slow, steady cooking. Woodstoves offer just that—a good, consistent heat – as long as the fire is maintained. Woodstoves are also great for baking. The wood smoke lends a wonderful flavor to anything cooked in the oven.

I light the stove at 4:30 am to have coffee and tea ready by 7 am. Lighting a fire in the stove is no different than lighting a campfire: use crumpled newspaper or leaves, lay small pieces of kindling on them first and then a little larger piece on top. Crisscross the kindling and open all the dampers to provide the oxygen necessary for a happy fire. The bigger logs don't go on until the fire is roaring happily. Once the fire gets started, the inertia is tough to stop.

People ask me all the time how I control the level of heat in a woodstove. When you want to increase the heat you give it more wood and more air; this means use smaller pieces of wood and open the dampers. When you want to reduce the heat, close the dampers and add big pieces of wood that will take longer to burn. One of the biggest challenges to cooking on a woodstove on a boat is that the apparent wind makes a big difference. How much wood the stove needs on a downwind day is completely different from how much it needs on a day we are tacking.

The heat on the stovetop is uneven; it's warmer by the firebox (where the fire is), cooler farther away. Because I can't just turn down the temperature on a woodstove, I adjust the heat by moving the pots to the warmer or cooler spots depending on how much heat I need at the moment. The same goes for the oven – I'm constantly turning the pans and shifting them from the upper shelf to the lower, closer to the firebox then farther away. The biggest challenge when using the oven is to get the insides done before the top or the bottom burns. And I never forget that the whole stove gets hot!

Fish

A cookbook about a Maine windjammer wouldn't be complete without addressing the bounty of the sea. Every morning, sometimes even before I'm up, I can hear lobster boats leaving the harbor to go fishing for the day. Their colorful buoys dot the bay. Our working waterfronts are an integral part of Maine's way of life. Rockland, Maine, our homeport, is a unique harbor in that it has a strong working waterfront, but also has space for 500 yacht moorings in the summer. We buy our fish from Jess's Market every week.

Caribbean Spiced Fish

The kind of fish you use is less important than the process. Any firm grilling fish with take well to this technique. Snapper, tuna and swordfish would be the best.

2 pounds of snapper, tuna or swordfish
Caribbean rub:
$^1/_2$ teaspoon cloves
1 teaspoon allspice
1 tablespoon freshly grated ginger
3 cloves garlic, minced
$^1/_2$ cup pineapple juice
Juice of 1 or 2 limes
Salt and pepper to taste

* Mix together all the ingredients but the fish.
* Rub the mixture liberally on both sides of the fish.
* Grill the fish until you can see it is cooked a little more than half way up the side (about five minutes).
* Turn carefully and continue cooking on the other side; the second side won't take as long (about 3 minutes).

Clam Sauce

$^1/_4$ cup ($^1/_2$ stick) butter
2 large onions, chopped
6 cloves garlic, minced
$^1/_4$ teaspoon salt
Several grinds on the pepper mill
1 cup white wine
2 14-ounce cans diced tomatoes
1 6-ounce can tomato paste
1 8-ounce bottle clam juice
1 10-ounce can chopped clams
2 tablespoons butter
Grated Parmesan cheese and minced parsley for garnish

* Melt the butter in a medium-sized stockpot over medium-high heat
* Add the onions, garlic, salt and pepper and cook until translucent.
* Add wine, tomatoes, tomato paste and clam juice, bring to a boil, reduce heat and simmer, uncovered, for 45 minutes.
* Add clams and cook until they are heated through, about 3 to 5 minutes.
* Remove from heat and add the butter, stirring until it is incorporated.
* Serve on top of your favorite pasta, garnished with the Parmesan cheese and parsley.

Curried Mussels

This one is great. Mussels aren't my favorite, but I really like them this way. You can serve the mussels alone as an appetizer or over pasta as a main course.

6 cloves garlic, minced
$^1/_4$ cup ($^1/_2$ stick) butter
$1^1/_2$ pounds mussels (in the shell)
$1^1/_2$ teaspoons curry
$^1/_2$ teaspoon salt
A few grinds on the pepper mill
$^1/_2$ cup white wine
$^1/_2$ cup heavy cream
3 scallions, thinly sliced

✳ Melt the butter in a medium-sized saucepan over medium heat and cook the garlic until soft.

✳ Add the mussels, curry, salt and pepper and stir everything together.

✳ Add the white wine and stir briefly.

✳ Add the heavy cream, cover and simmer until the mussels are done (when the shells open – about 5 to 10 minutes).

✳ Garnish with the sliced scallions.

Haddock with Herbed Butter, Caramelized Onions and Tomatoes

Serves 4

Herbed Butter:

1 cup (2 sticks) unsalted butter, softened
$^1/_2$ cup loosely packed basil
$^1/_2$ cup loosely packed parsley
$^1/_2$ shallot
1 small clove garlic
$^1/_2$ teaspoon salt
$^1/_8$ teaspoon pepper

Caramelized Onions:

1 tablespoon butter
2 large onions, sliced
$^1/_2$ teaspoon salt
$^1/_4$ teaspoon freshly ground black pepper
2 tablespoons fresh thyme leaves, or 1 teaspoon dried
2 pounds haddock
3 tomatoes, sliced

* Make the herbed butter by processing the softened butter, basil, parsley, shallot, garlic, salt and pepper together.
* Turn the butter on to a piece of plastic wrap and form the butter into a log. Wrap it in the plastic wrap and chill or freeze.
* Heat the butter and oil in a medium skillet over medium-low heat.
* Add the onions and cook until they begin to soften, stirring occasionally, about 15 minutes.
* Add the salt and pepper; raise heat slightly, and cook until golden brown, stirring occasionally, 30 to 35 minutes.
* Stir in the thyme.
* Preheat oven to 375°. Oil a 9 x 13-inch pan.
* Spread the onions in the bottom of the pan, then place the haddock on the onions.
* Cover the haddock with the sliced tomatoes.
* Bake until the haddock is still a tiny bit opaque in the middle (about 20 minutes). It will keep cooking when you remove it from the oven.
* Slice the herbed butter into $^1/_4$-inch medallions and place them on top of the tomatoes and serve.

Lemon Lobster with Sun-Dried Tomatoes   *Serves 2*

This recipe was a summer favorite at Jessica's Restaurant when I was a sous chef under Chef Hans Bucher. It's important to have all the ingredients ready and on hand before you start. Don't start this one until the pasta is in the water and you've given it a good stir.

> 1 tablespoon butter
> 2 teaspoons shallots, minced
> 8 ounces cooked lobster meat (approximately one $1^1/_2$ pound lobster)
> $^1/_4$ cup sun-dried tomatoes in oil, oil drained, chopped
> $^1/_4$ teaspoon salt
> A few grinds on the pepper mill
> $^1/_3$ cup white wine
> Juice of $^1/_2$ lemon
> 1 tablespoon butter
> Grated Parmesan cheese and minced parsley for garnish

* Melt the butter in a large sauté pan over medium-high heat.
* Add the sun-dried tomatoes; sauté for one minute, then add the shallots and cook until soft.
* When the shallots are done add the lobster meat and sauté for 1 minute.
* Add the white wine and lemon juice; cook for another 30 seconds and remove from heat.
* Gently stir in the butter until it's completely incorporated.
* Serve over pasta and garnish with the cheese and parsley.

Pommery Mussels

You can serve the mussels alone as an appetizer or over pasta as a main course.

2 tablespoons butter
1 tablespoon minced shallots
1 tablespoon Pommery mustard
$1^1/_2$ pounds mussels
$^3/_4$ cup white wine
Juice of $^1/_2$ lemon
1 cup diced, peeled, and seeded fresh tomatoes
$^1/_2$ teaspoon salt

* Melt the butter in a medium-sized saucepan over medium-high heat.
* Add the shallots; sauté until tender.
* Add the mustard and sauté briefly.
* Add the remaining ingredients, stir briefly, cover and reduce heat medium-low and simmer until the mussels have opened (about 5-10 minutes).

Sesame Seared Tuna

4-6 fresh tuna fillets
$^1/_2$ cup soy sauce
3 cloves garlic, minced
1 tablespoon peeled and grated fresh ginger
1 tablespoon lime juice
3 tablespoons toasted sesame oil
$^1/_2$ cup sesame seeds
2 tablespoons olive oil

✳ Marinate the tuna in everything except the sesame seeds and olive oil for one hour.
✳ Heat a large sauté pan on medium-high heat for a minute or two.
✳ Drizzle the olive oil into the pan and then sprinkle the sesame seeds evenly in the pan.
✳ Gently place the tuna steaks on top of the sesame seeds and cook for 1 to 4 minutes on each side (depending on how well done you like your tuna and how thick the tuna is). Don't forget that they will continue cooking after you take them out of the pan so remove them a little less done than you would like.
✳ Serve on top of Sautéed Greens

Salmon with Tri-Pepper Salsa

This is a great one. Everyone loves it – even folks who normally don't like salmon.

A note about the julienned peppers for the salsa: the strips shouldn't be too long; if they are, cut them in half cross-wise. This is mostly a practical thing. If they are too long you end up sticking them in your nose when you try to eat them.

Salsa:

$^1/_2$ red bell pepper, seeded, cut in half lengthwise, and julienned
$^1/_2$ green bell pepper, seeded, cut in half lengthwise, and julienned
$^1/_2$ yellow bell pepper, seeded, cut in half lengthwise, and julienned
1 red onion, cut in half and thinly sliced
3 tablespoons extra-virgin olive oil
Juice of $1^1/_2$ limes
2 tablespoons fresh dill, chopped
$^1/_2$ teaspoon salt
Freshly ground pepper

Salmon:

4 to 6 salmon filets
1 teaspoon salt
Freshly ground black pepper
4 tablespoons fresh lemon juice
4 tablespoons extra-virgin olive oil
4 tablespoons white wine

Prepare the salsa:

✳ Toss the veggies with the olive oil, lime juice, and dill.
✳ Add salt and pepper to taste; let the salsa sit at room temperature for an hour (two at the most – you don't want it to get soggy). Check the seasoning again just before you serve.

Prepare the salmon:

✳ Preheat oven to 375°.
✳ Put the salmon in a 9 x 13-inch baking pan, preferably a non-reactive one – enamel or ceramic.
✳ Drizzle the lemon juice, olive oil and white wine over the salmon and season with salt and pepper.
✳ Let the salmon sit for 15 minutes, then bake, uncovered, for about 15 to 20 minutes.

✳ Take the fish out when it is still somewhat darker pink in the center. It will continue to cook once you take it out of the oven so take it out before it's quite done.

✳ Serve the salsa on top of the salmon.

Shrimp with Prosciutto and Green Olives on Fettuccini
Serves 2

This is a recipe that came from three years of working with Hans Bucher, my mentor. This was one of his wife's favorite combinations; he served it with pasta or risotto. Sometimes we would wrap the shrimp in Prosciutto and grill it while making the sauce with the olives.

Enough fettuccini for two people
1 tablespoon butter
2 slices Prosciutto, diced
$^1/_3$ cup pitted green olives
1 tablespoon garlic, minced
1 pound shrimp, peeled and deveined
$^1/_3$ cup white wine
Juice of half a lemon
1 tablespoon butter
Grated Parmesan cheese and minced parsley to garnish

* Prepare the fettuccini as you normally would; when it is about 5 minutes away from being done, melt the butter in a large sauté pan over medium-high heat.
* Add the olives and Prosciutto and sauté for one minute.
* Add the garlic and sauté for 30 seconds.
* Add the shrimp and sauté until it is nearly cooked through, about 2 minutes (depending on the size).
* Add the white wine and lemon juice and continue to cook for 30 seconds.
* Remove the pan from the heat and gently stir in butter until it's all incorporated.
* Drain the fettuccini.
* Spoon the shrimp over the fettuccini and garnish with the Parmesan cheese and parsley.

Meat

These are a sample of the dinner menus I serve on board the *Riggin*. The actual menus vary based on what's available from the farm, the weather, and my imagination!

* Roasted Mushroom and Artichoke Sauce, Roasted Garlic, Parmesan Cheese, Risotto, garden salad, with Lemon Parmesan Dressing, Crusty Peasant Bread, Chocolate Decadence Pie

* Chicken Curry with Couscous, Cantaloupe Raita and condiments (bananas, apples, nuts, coconut, peppers, onions, raisins and hard-boiled eggs), Jim's Raisin Bread, steamed broccoli, Blueberry Pie

* Riggin Rib Roast with Horseradish Cream, Yorkshire Pudding, Rosemary Potatoes, steamed carrots and broccoli, Pumpkin Cheesecake

* Chicken Paprika with sour cream, Polenta, Crusty Peasant Bread with Caramelized Onions, garden salad with Dana's Maple-Dill Dressing, Apricot-Ginger Pound Cake with Rum Glaze

* Riggin Ham with Roasted Onions, Cinnamon Roasted Sweet Potatoes, steamed green beans with almonds, Cheddar Cheese Biscuits, Black Bottom Banana Cream Pie

* Pork Loin with Cranberry Port Sauce, Barley Risotto with mushrooms, Sautéed Greens, roasted beets, Whole Wheat Walnut Bread, Carrot-Banana Cake

* Fettuccini with Clam Sauce, Roasted Garlic, Parmesan Cheese, garden salad, Blue Cheese Dressing, Focaccia, Fresh Lime Pie

Black Forest Pork Stew

2 tablespoons olive oil
2 pounds pork stew meat
$^1/_4$ cup flour
1 teaspoon salt
$^1/_2$ teaspoon freshly ground pepper
1 teaspoon paprika
3 slices bacon, diced
2 large onions, diced
4 large carrots, diced
3 stalks celery, diced
9 cloves garlic, minced
2 tablespoons fresh minced marjoram
6 ounces tomato paste
1 cup white wine
2 cups beef stock or water
1 teaspoon salt
$^1/_2$ teaspoon freshly ground pepper
1 pound bratwurst, cut into 1-inch pieces
1 8-ounce package mushrooms, washed and quartered

* Heat the olive oil in a stockpot over medium-high heat.
* Toss the pork, flour, salt, pepper and paprika together in a bowl to coat the meat.
* Add the pork to the pot and cook until lightly browned.
* Add the bacon and continue cooking until the bacon is done (about 5 minutes).
* Add the onions, carrots, celery, garlic and spices and cook for another 10-15 minutes until the onions are translucent.
* Add the tomato paste, white wine, stock, salt, pepper and bratwurst. Reduce heat and simmer, covered, until the meat is tender (about 2 hours).
* Add the mushrooms and cook an additional 15 minutes; serve.

Bolognese Sauce

Serves 4 to 6

1 tablespoon olive oil
$^1/_2$ pound ground beef
1 teaspoon salt
$^1/_2$ teaspoon fresh pepper
1 large onion, diced
$^1/_2$ green pepper, seeded and diced
9 cloves garlic, minced
$1^1/_2$ tablespoons fresh minced basil
3 tablespoons fresh minced thyme
3 tablespoons fresh minced marjoram
3 tablespoons fresh minced oregano
1 teaspoon salt
4 ounces mushrooms, washed and quartered
2 28-ounce cans diced tomatoes
2 cups red wine

✳ Heat the olive oil in a large pot over medium heat.

✳ Brown the ground beef with the salt and pepper.

✳ Add the onions, pepper, garlic, spices and salt and cook until tender and translucent.

✳ Add the remaining ingredients; reduce heat, cover, and simmer 2 hours.

Meatloaf

Serves 6

This is my mom's recipe. As a little girl I loved the leftover meatloaf sandwiches more than the meal itself.

2 pounds ground beef
1 cup oatmeal or breadcrumbs
1 cup tomato juice or $^2/_3$ cup milk
1 large egg
3 tablespoons ketchup
2 tablespoons grated onion
2 tablespoons fresh chopped parsley
Salt and pepper to taste

✳ Preheat oven to 350°.

✳ Mix it all up, pat it into a greased loaf pan and pop it into the oven.

✳ Bake for 1 hour. Let it cool at least 15 minutes before serving.

Bunny Overboard!

When an errant hat flies off of someone's head and into the water, we often take this as an opportunity for a "man overboard" drill: getting into our positions, rescuing the hat, and recording our time.

When Chlöe was little she had three little stuffed bunnies that she loved to play with. As any parent knows, the loss of a favorite friend is a big deal, and going to some lengths to replace or rescue this friend is worth the effort. One day, one of the bunnies decided to take a trip over the rail. Chlöe was devastated. Jon quickly called "bunny overboard!" and with the help of the passengers and crew we retrieved the slightly salty bunny in record time.

Braised Lamb Shanks with Thyme, Cinnamon and Fennel

Serves 4

4 lamb shanks, $^3/_4$- to 1-pound each
2 tablespoons vegetable oil
1 tablespoon butter
3 medium onions, chopped
2 large carrots, chopped
2 large parsnips, chopped
4 large fresh thyme sprigs
2 whole garlic heads; unpeeled, cut in half horizontally
1 cup dry red wine
5 cups chicken stock
1 large orange, peeled, quartered and pith cut away
2 whole cinnamon sticks
1 teaspoon fennel seeds, crushed
2 tablespoons butter

* Preheat oven to 375°.
* Season the lamb with salt and pepper.
* Heat the oil in large, heavy-duty, ovenproof pot over high heat.
* Add the lamb and cook until brown on all sides (about 10 minutes).
* Remove the lamb and keep warm.
* Add the butter to the drippings in the pot.
* Add the onion, carrots, parsnips, thyme, and garlic. Sauté until the vegetables soften and begin to brown, about 8 minutes.
* Add the wine and boil until the liquid is reduced almost to a glaze, about 4 minutes.
* Return the lamb shanks to the pot, arranging them in a single layer.
* Add the stock, orange, cinnamon sticks, and fennel seeds; bring to boil.
* Place the pot in the oven and cook, uncovered, until tender, turning and basting often (about 2 hours 15 minutes).
* Transfer the lamb to a plate and keep warm.
* Strain the braising liquid into a bowl and spoon off the fat.
* Return the liquid to the pot. Simmer until the sauce is thick enough to coat the back of a spoon, about 15 minutes.
* Return the lamb to the pot; cover and warm over medium-low heat 10 to 15 minutes, until the lamb is completely reheated. Serve.

Curried Lamb and Lentil Stew

Serves 4-6

2 tablespoons olive oil
1$^1/_2$ pounds lamb stew meat
2 large onions, chopped
2 large carrots, chopped
6 cloves garlic, minced
1 tablespoon grated ginger
1 teaspoon salt
$^1/_2$ teaspoon fresh pepper
2 tablespoons curry powder
1 cup red wine
3 cups beef stock
3 medium potatoes, peeled and chopped into   -inch cubes
1 cup French lentils

✳ Heat the olive oil in a large pot over medium-high heat.
✳ Season the lamb with salt and pepper and cook until browned.
✳ Add the onions, carrots, garlic, ginger, curry, salt and pepper and cook until the onions are translucent (about 10 minutes).
✳ Add the red wine and beef stock. Cover, reduce heat and simmer until the meat is nearly tender (about 1   hours). Add the potatoes and lentils and more stock if needed and continue to simmer until the potatoes and lentils are cooked (about 25 minutes).
✳ Serve over polenta.

Riggin Ham

A large ham will serve 20 people. I usually buy two medium-sized hams. Look for hams without the labels "ham, water added" or "ham and water product." Ham is actually a fairly low-fat cut of meat; high in salt, but low in fat. You can't have everything.

1 ham, cured and fully cooked
Red pepper jelly (see From the Pantry)
8 large onions, peeled and cut into eighths

✳ Preheat oven to 350°.
✳ Place the ham alone in a roasting pan and roast for 1 hour.
✳ Add the onions; roast for another hour.
✳ Remove the ham from the oven. If the onions are soft and golden, remove them. If not, continue to roast them with the ham.
✳ Trim the excess fat to $\frac{1}{4}$-inch, then cut scores $\frac{1}{4}$-inch deep across the ham. Spread the red pepper jelly liberally over the ham.
✳ Return the ham to the oven, basting frequently, until the jelly is golden brown (about 20 minutes).
✳ Allow the ham to rest at least 15 minutes before serving.

Six Days a Week

If you check our sailing schedule you'll notice that we offer primarily six-day trips. That's because something magical happens on a six-day trip that doesn't happen on shorter trips. It's something we see again and again – worried faces relax, watches are taken off, real conversations start, and life starts to center on the Here and Now. Folks are changed by the end of a week. They are calmer, their shoulders have dropped two inches and they are laughing – a lot. Repeat passengers that take a shorter trip say the experience is not the same – the trip is just too short. Jon and I and our crew have also seen this, which is why we offer as many six-day trips as possible.

110

Beef Ragu with Fennel and Orange   *Serves 4-6*

2 tablespoons olive oil
2 pounds stew beef
$1/4$ cup flour
1 teaspoon salt
$1/2$ teaspoon freshly ground pepper
1 teaspoon paprika
1 large onion, diced
1 cup diced fennel
2 large carrots, diced
3 stalks celery, diced
$1/2$ green pepper, diced
6 cloves minced garlic
2 tablespoons fennel seed
$1/2$ tablespoon ground cinnamon
1 tablespoon dried thyme
1 teaspoon salt
$1/2$ teaspoon freshly ground pepper
Zest of one orange
2 cups red wine
1 14-ounce can diced tomatoes

Heat the olive oil in a large pot over medium-high heat.
Toss the beef, flour, salt, pepper and paprika in a bowl so the beef is coated
   with the flour.
Place the beef in the pot and cook until browned.
Add the onions, fennel, carrots, celery, peppers, garlic, spices, salt and cook
   for another 10-15 minutes until the onions are translucent.
Add the orange zest, red wine and tomatoes. Cover, reduce heat and
   simmer for 2 hours or until the meat is tender.
Serve with polenta.

Riggin Rib Roast with Horseradish Cream *Serves 6-8*

No rib roast would be complete without Yorkshire pudding (see Sides).

Rib Roast (bone-in), about $4^1/_2$ to 6 pounds
$^1/_2$ teaspoon salt
$^1/_4$ teaspoon freshly ground black pepper
$^1/_2$ teaspoon paprika
1 tablespoon Dijon mustard
Three cloves garlic, minced
1 tablespoon chopped fresh rosemary

* Preheat oven to 425°.
* Place roast in a roasting pan, fat side up; rub the roast with salt, pepper and paprika.
* Place the roast into the oven, reduce heat to 325° and cook for 1 to $1^1/_2$ hours.
* Rub the roast with the remaining ingredients; return it to the oven and continue to roast to the desired temperature until the internal temperature of the meat reads 120° for rare, 125° for medium-rare, 130° for medium, and 135° for well done.
* Remove the roast from the oven and let it rest 10 minutes before slicing. The internal heat of the beef will cause it to continue to cook another 10 degrees.
* While the roast is resting, make the Horseradish Cream, below.

Horseradish Cream

The amount of salt you use will vary depending on whether you use bottled or fresh horseradish.

3 tablespoons bottled horseradish or 1 tablespoon grated fresh
Salt as needed
Freshly ground black pepper as needed
Juice of half a lemon
1 cup heavy cream, whipped to soft peaks

* Mix all the ingredients except the whipped cream together.
* Gently fold in the whipped cream and serve.

"Lamb"sagna

Serves 6-8

I created this recipe exclusively for Agricola Farms. We get all our lamb from them and it's wonderful.

2 tablespoons olive oil
1 pound ground lamb
$^1/_2$ teaspoon salt
1 large onion, diced
6 cloves garlic, chopped
2 tablespoons chopped fresh basil, or 1 dried
2 tablespoons all-purpose flour
1 cup milk
4 zucchini or summer squash, sliced long wise
2 tablespoons olive oil (more if needed)
$^1/_4$ teaspoon salt
4 large tomatoes, sliced
1$^1/_2$ cups breadcrumbs
1 cup feta cheese, crumbled

✳ Preheat oven to 350°.
✳ Heat the oil in a medium saucepan over medium-high heat.
✳ Brown the lamb with the salt.
✳ Add the onion, garlic and basil. When the onion is translucent, sprinkle in the flour and stir for a minute or so. Add the milk and bring it to a simmer.
✳ Remove from heat.
✳ Heat the olive oil in a separate sauté pan. Add the sliced zucchini and summer squash and sauté until brown. Set aside.
✳ Layer half of the lamb, then half of the squash, then half the tomatoes in an ungreased 9 x 13-inch baking pan. Repeat with the remaining lamb and squash
✳ Evenly sprinkle breadcrumbs and feta cheese over the squash.
✳ Bake, uncovered, until the cheese is brown and bubbling (about 45 minutes).
✳ Remove from oven and cool 10 minutes before serving.

What Counter Space?

The galley of the Riggin has about 3 feet of counter space (give or take a few inches). I'm often asked how I manage to prepare meals for 30 people all summer long on such a small space. One passenger, whose wife was angling for a new kitchen, even came to measure the exact amount of counter space so he could use this information as his rebuttal.

I am not by nature a terribly organized person, but cooking well requires that you have all your ingredients on hand and prepared before you start cooking. Chefs call it "mise en place". This takes a level of stress away and insures consistent success. It helps that my mess cook does a lot of the chopping and cutting, as well as a number of passengers.

Any leftover meat and veggies can be cut up and cooked into a hash.

1 brisket corned beef (about 6 pounds)
1 pound package carrots, peeled and cut into 1 -inch chunks
12 to 16 small red potatoes, skin on
12 to 16 small white onions, peeled
1 large turnip, peeled and cut into 1 -inch chunks
1 large head of cabbage, cored and cut into eight wedges

✳ Place the corned beef in a large stew pot and cover with water. Cover, bring to a boil, reduce heat, and simmer until fork tender (2 to 3 hours).
✳ Remove the meat from the pot. DO NOT drain the water.
✳ Place the potatoes and turnip in the pot, bring the water back to a boil and simmer 15 minutes.
✳ Add the carrots and onions, bring to a boil and simmer another 10 minutes.
✳ Add the cabbage, bring to a boil and simmer another 5 minutes.
✳ Strain all the vegetables into a colander.
✳ Slice the beef diagonally against the grain; arrange the meat and vegetables on a platter and serve with Mustard Sauce (below) and Irish Soda Bread.

Mustard Sauce

2 tablespoons dry mustard
1 teaspoon all-purpose flour
$^1/_2$ teaspoon salt
1 can evaporated milk
$^1/_4$ cup sugar
1 large egg yolk
$^1/_2$ cup heated cider vinegar

✳ Mix together the mustard, flour and salt. Add $^1/_3$ cup of evaporated milk and whisk until there are no lumps.
✳ Put the sugar and the rest of the evaporated milk in a double boiler over medium heat.
✳ Whisk in the mustard mixture, then whisk in the egg yolks.
✳ Heat, whisking frequently, until the mixture thickens to a ribbon-like consistency.
✳ Remove the mixture from the heat and whisk in the heated vinegar. Leave it in the double boiler until you're ready to serve to keep warm.
✳ Pour into a pitcher and serve.

Mom's Spaghetti with Meat Balls

This is the meal that as kids we would ask for more than any other. It was our favorite birthday dinner for many years.

Sauce:

1 28-ounce can of pureed tomatoes
1 28-ounce can of crushed or diced tomatoes
1 12-ounce can tomato paste
1 teaspoon salt
1 teaspoon sugar
$1/4$ teaspoon dried oregano
$1/4$ teaspoon dried basil
$1/4$ teaspoon crushed red pepper
1 large onion, diced
2 tablespoons parsley flakes

Meat Balls:

2 pounds ground beef
1 cup breadcrumbs
1 teaspoon salt
$1/2$ teaspoon dried oregano
2 cloves minced garlic
$1/8$ teaspoon fresh black pepper
1 large egg

Sauce:

* Add everything to a stockpot, bring to a boil, reduce heat, and simmer, uncovered, for 2 hours, stirring occasionally.
* While the sauce is simmering make the meatballs.

Meatballs:

* Preheat oven to 350°.
* Mix together the meatball ingredients. Form them into $1^1/_2$-inch balls.
* Place the meatballs in a single layer in a baking pan. Bake until cooked through (around $1/_2$ hour).
* Drain off the fat and place the meatballs into the sauce and simmer for another 30 minutes.
* Serve with your favorite spaghetti or linguini.

Pork Loin with Cranberry Port Sauce   *Serves 4-6*

You'll need to start this the day before (for the pork marinade).

3 pounds boneless pork loin
$^3/_4$ cup chopped fresh parsley
3 tablespoons chopped fresh rosemary
$^3/_4$ cup chopped fresh sage
2 teaspoons salt
$^1/_2$ teaspoon freshly ground black pepper
$^1/_4$ cup olive oil

✳ Combine all the ingredients except the pork. Rub the pork loin all over with the herb mixture; cover and refrigerate overnight.
✳ Preheat oven to 375°.
✳ Place the pork in a roasting pan and roast until the internal temperature of the meat reaches 145° for medium and 150° for medium well, (about 1 hour).
✳ Remove the pork from the oven and let it rest, covered, for 10 minutes.
✳ Slice and serve with the Cranberry Port Sauce, below.

Cranberry Port Sauce

$^1/_2$ pound fresh cranberries
6 tablespoons port
6 tablespoons sugar
2 tablespoons orange juice
$^1/_2$ tablespoon grated orange zest
$^1/_8$-inch thick slice of fresh ginger
1 tablespoon red currant jelly

✳ Combine the cranberries, port, sugar, orange juice, orange zest, and ginger in a small enamel (or other non-reactive) saucepan.
✳ Bring the mixture to a boil over medium-high heat, stirring to dissolve the sugar.
✳ Reduce heat to low and simmer for 12 to 15 minutes, stirring frequently, until the cranberries have popped and the sauce is slightly thickened.
✳ Discard the gingerroot, stir in the jelly, and set aside to cool slightly.
✳ Pour the sauce into a pitcher and serve with the sliced pork. It's great, hot, cold, or room temperature.

2 tablespoons olive oil
1 pound pork stew meat
1 cup chopped fennel
2 large onions, chopped
2 large carrots, chopped
2 tablespoons chopped fresh sage (or 1 teaspoon dried)
2 tablespoons minced fresh rosemary (or 1 tablespoon dried)
2 tablespoons minced garlic
1 teaspoon salt
$1/_2$ teaspoon fresh black pepper
$1/_2$ cup all-purpose flour
2 tablespoons tomato paste
6 cups beef stock
1 sheet puff pastry
Oil as needed to brush on the pastry.

* Heat the olive oil in a large pot over medium-high heat.
* Place the pork in the pot and cook until browned.
* Add the fennel, onions, carrots, garlic, herbs, salt and pepper and cook for another 10-15 minutes until the onions are translucent.
* Dust with the flour, stir, and add the tomato paste. Stir frequently for about 2 minutes.
* Add the beef stock; cover, reduce heat and simmer for $1^1/_2$ to 2 hours or until the meat is nearly done.
* Spoon the mixture into a 9 x 13-inch ovenproof ceramic dish.
* Rub the edge of the pan with water and cover it with the pastry dough. Press down on the edges to seal the pastry to the edge of the pan and brush the pastry with oil.
* Bake at 350° for 45 minutes.
* Allow the pie to rest for 10 minutes before serving.

Pork Tenderloin with Creamy Caper Sauce   *Serves 2*

This sauce is also wonderful with chicken or salmon.

1 pork tenderloin
$^1/_2$ teaspoon freshly ground black pepper
$^1/_2$ teaspoon salt
$^1/_2$ teaspoon paprika
1 medium onion, chopped
2 cloves garlic, minced
$^1/_4$ teaspoon salt
1 tomato, peeled, seeded and chopped
1 teaspoon fresh minced basil
1 teaspoon fresh minced tarragon
$^1/_4$ cup white wine
1 to 2 tablespoons water or vegetable stock
$^1/_2$ cup heavy cream
2 tablespoons capers
3 to 4 tablespoons vegetable or chicken stock

✳ Preheat oven to 350°.
✳ Rub the tenderloin with the salt, pepper, and paprika.
✳ Heat the oil in a large ovenproof sauté pan over medium-high heat.
✳ Add the pork tenderloin and brown it on all sides.
✳ Reduce heat to medium; add the onions, garlic, and salt and cook until the onions are translucent. Turn the tenderloin occasionally while the onions are cooking.
✳ Add the tomatoes and herbs and cook for another minute.
✳ Add the wine, stock and heavy cream and bring to a simmer.
✳ Place the sauté pan in the oven and cook until the pork reaches internal temperature of is 145° for medium and 150° for medium well, about 10 minutes.
✳ Remove from oven. Set aside the tenderloin and puree the sauce until smooth
✳ Add the capers.
✳ Cut the tenderloin on an angle into   to -inch slices and serve with the sauce.

Sautéed Beef Tenderloin Filets with Port and Mushroom Sauce

Serves 4

4 8-ounce beef tenderloin filets
3 tablespoons olive oil
$^1/_4$ teaspoon salt
$^1/_4$ teaspoon freshly ground black pepper
1 tablespoon butter
1 tablespoon minced shallots
$^1/_2$ teaspoon Worcestershire
3 tablespoons port
3 tablespoons butter
8 ounces mushrooms, thinly sliced

✳ Marinate the filets in the oil, salt and pepper half an hour.
✳ While the tenderloins are marinating, heat a large sauté pan over medium-high heat until hot (about 2 minutes).
✳ Sauté the tenderloins on both sides until they are nearly cooked to the temperature you want; 125° for rare, 130° for medium-rare, 135° for medium, and 140° for well done (they'll continue to cook for a few minutes after you've removed them from the pan).
✳ Remove the tenderloins, cover them with foil and set them aside to keep warm.
✳ Add the butter and shallots to the same sauté pan; reduce heat to medium and sauté for 30 seconds to a minute.
✳ Add the mushrooms and sauté them until they are nearly cooked through.
✳ Whisk in the port and the Worcestershire sauce; heat it until mixture starts to simmer.
✳ Remove the pan from the heat and gently whisk in the butter.
✳ Spoon the liquid onto a platter, place the beef on top of the sauce and then spoon the mushrooms onto the beef.

The Details and Variations:

What you just made was a butter sauce. It's a very delicate sauce, meaning that it breaks easily, so it's important to put the butter into the pan after you've removed the pan from the heat; if it comes to a boil it will break.

You can use this recipe as a base and add all sorts of ingredients to change the flavor of the sauce. Most of these will work together: choose two or three and be brave!

Variations:
Peppercorns
Tomatoes
Lemon juice
Caramelized onions
Fresh minced chives and parsley
Chopped black Kalamata olives

Three Sausage and Butternut Squash Sauce Serves 12-16

I created this recipe exclusively for Curtis Custom Meats in Union, Maine. They are wonderful – we buy most of our meat from them. This makes a large pot of sauce – enough that you can serve it once, and freeze the rest for another time.

1 butternut squash, peeled, seeded and cut into -inch pieces
2 tablespoons olive oil
$^1/_2$ teaspoon salt
$^1/_4$ teaspoon fresh pepper
2 tablespoons olive oil
1 pound hot sausage, cut into 1-inch slices
1 pound sweet sausage, cut into 1-inch slices
1 pound garlic sausage, cut into 1-inch slices
3 large onions, chopped
6 cloves garlic, minced
4 tablespoons fresh basil, or 2 tablespoons dried
3 tablespoons Italian seasoning
1 cup red wine
6 cups peeled, seeded, and diced tomatoes (or 2 16-ounce cans diced tomatoes)
$^1/_2$ teaspoon salt
Ricotta cheese and fresh chopped parsley to garnish

✳ Preheat oven to 500°.
✳ Toss the squash with the olive oil, salt, and pepper and roast for 45 minutes or until the squash is cooked through (but not falling apart).
✳ Heat the olive oil in a large stockpot over medium-high heat.
✳ Add the sausages and sauté until they are lightly browned.
✳ Add the onions, garlic, and seasonings and continue to cook until the onions are translucent.
✳ Add the wine, tomatoes and salt; reduce heat and simmer for at least 30 minutes.
✳ Add the squash and serve over your favorite pasta and garnish with the ricotta cheese and parsley.

Zucchini and Genoa Salami Deep Dish Pizza *Serves 8-12*

2 tablespoons olive oil
2 zucchini, roughly chopped
2 summer squash, roughly chopped
$^1/_2$ teaspoon salt
$^1/_2$ teaspoon pepper
1 cup grated Parmesan cheese
1 pound Genoa salami, cut in medium-thick slices
1 cup mozzarella, grated
2 cups whole milk ricotta cheese
1 Crusty Peasant bread dough recipe. You can also use the pre-made bread dough you can find in most grocery stores – you'll need 2 bags.
Olive oil to brush over the crust
Dried basil, Italian seasoning, oregano - whatever you like – to sprinkle on the crust

✳ Oil a 9 x 13-inch baking pan.

✳ Heat the olive oil in a large sauté pan over medium-high heat

✳ Add the zucchini, summer squash, salt and pepper. Sauté until tender.

✳ Divide the dough roughly in half; make one part slightly larger than the other.

✳ Either roll or use your hands to stretch the larger piece until it's big enough to overlap over the sides of the baking pan by about 1 inch.

✳ Spread half of the Parmesan cheese evenly over the dough. Add layers (in order) of half each of the salami, mozzarella, ricotta, zucchini and summer squash. When you transfer the squash to the pizza, use a slotted spoon to drain the excess liquid. Repeat.

✳ Stretch the remaining half of the dough out enough to overlap the top of the pan, then pinch the two layers of dough together neatly.

✳ Brush the crust with the olive oil and sprinkle with the herbs.

✳ Preheat oven to 350°.

✳ Let the pizza rest and rise for 30 minutes, then bake until golden brown (about an hour).

✳ Cool 15 minutes before cutting and serving.

Poultry

Chicken And Winter Veggie Stew *Serves 6*

This stew is wonderful with either biscuits or garlic-mashed potatoes.

2 tablespoons olive oil
3 pounds of boneless, skinless chicken breasts or thighs, cut into 2-inch pieces
1 teaspoon salt
$^1/_2$ teaspoon freshly ground pepper
1 teaspoon paprika
1 large onion, coarsely chopped
9 cloves minced garlic
1 tablespoon minced fresh tarragon
1 tablespoon minced fresh thyme
4 carrots, coarsely chopped
4 parsnips, peeled and coarsely chopped
$^1/_4$ cup all-purpose flour
1 cup white wine
4 to 6 cups chicken broth
$1^1/_2$ cups frozen peas
6 ounces (small package) button mushrooms, cleaned and quartered

✳ Heat the oil in a large pot over medium-high heat.
✳ Brown the chicken on all sides and set aside.
✳ To the same pan, add the salt, pepper, paprika, onions, garlic, herbs, carrots and parsnips and cook until the onions are translucent.
✳ Sprinkle the flour into the pan; stir.
✳ Add the wine, chicken broth and chicken and stir; bring to a boil, reduce heat, and simmer, uncovered, until the meat is tender (about an hour).
✳ Fifteen minutes before serving, add the peas and the mushrooms.
✳ Serve with biscuits or potatoes and a salad.

Chicken Curry

On board ship, sailors would use the spices that they acquired in the Caribbean islands to flavor their food. Spices added flavor, but were also used for practical reasons – to cover the smell of less than fresh meat. With refrigeration that's certainly not a problem these days, but it's an interesting bit of history. The condiments we serve with the curry make a very festive presentation; the table overflows with bowls and platters. I usually serve it on the last night of the trip.

2 tablespoons olive oil
3 pounds boneless, skinless chicken thighs cut into 2-inch pieces
2 large onions, chopped
1 large green pepper, seeded and diced
$1/2$ jalapeno pepper, seeded and minced (optional)
3 cloves minced garlic
2 tablespoons freshly grated ginger
3 tablespoons curry powder
1 teaspoon cumin
1 teaspoon salt
1 14-ounce can diced tomatoes
1 can coconut milk
Juice of 1 lime

* Heat the oil in a large, wide stockpot over medium-high heat.
* Place the chicken in the pot and cook until browned on all sides.
* Add the onion, peppers, garlic, ginger, spices and salt; cook for another 10-15 minutes until the onions are translucent.
* Add the tomatoes and coconut milk; simmer, uncovered, 45 minutes or until chicken is tender. Add water if needed.
* Serve over couscous or rice, with any of the condiments below and/or the Cantaloupe Raita (recipe below).

Cantaloupe Raita

Raita is typically yogurt and cucumbers, used to "cool down" the spiciness of the curry. I use cantaloupe as a twist.

1 cup diced cantaloupe
2 cups yogurt
1 tablespoon minced fresh cilantro
$1/4$ teaspoon salt
Freshly ground black pepper to taste

* Mix everything together. Serve immediately.

Condiments:
Chopped bananas or apples
Chopped peanuts
Chopped hardboiled eggs
Chopped green and red peppers
Chopped onions
Shredded coconut
Lime wedges
Raisins

Chicken Paprika

   If you plan to freeze or refrigerate this dish to serve later, leave out the sour cream. When you reheat it, add the sour cream just before serving. It won't curdle if you freeze it and it will keep longer if you refrigerate it.

> 2 tablespoons olive oil
> 3 pounds of boneless, skinless chicken (thighs or breasts)
> 1 teaspoon salt
> $^1/_4$ teaspoon pepper
> 2 large onions, chopped
> 1 large green pepper, seeded and diced
> 3 cloves garlic, minced
> 2 tablespoons paprika
> $^1/_4$ cup tomato paste
> 2 14-ounce cans diced tomatoes
> $^1/_2$ cup red wine
> Several dashes of Worcestershire
> 8 ounces mushrooms, quartered
> 1 cup sour cream

* Heat the oil in a large, wide stockpot over medium-high heat.
* Place the chicken, salt and pepper in the heated pot and cook until browned on all sides.
* Add the onions, peppers, garlic and paprika; cook for another 10-15 minutes until the onions are translucent.
* Add the tomato paste and cook, stirring, for about a minute.
* Add the wine, tomatoes and Worcestershire; cover and cook until the chicken is tender (about 45 minutes). Add water if needed.
* Add the mushrooms and cook another 5 minutes.
* Stir in the sour cream and serve with noodles, potatoes or polenta.

Cornish Game Hens with Smoked Shrimp and Brandy Stuffing

Serves 4

Stuffing:

2 tablespoons butter
1 small onion, minced
1 stalk celery, minced
$^1/_2$ minced shallot
$1^1/_2$ cups finely diced day old French bread
1 tablespoon brandy
$^1/_2$ cup chicken stock
$^3/_4$ cup smoked Ducktrap shrimp
$^1/_4$ teaspoon salt

Hens:

4 Cornish game hens
4 tablespoons olive oil
1 teaspoon salt
$^1/_2$ teaspoon pepper
1 teaspoon paprika

✳ Preheat oven to 375°.

✳ Heat a medium-sized sauté pan over medium heat.

✳ Add the butter and sauté the onion, celery, shallots and salt.

✳ Add the mixture to the remaining stuffing ingredients and gently toss until everything is mixed.

✳ Rub the outside and inside with the oil, salt, pepper and paprika. Stuff the hens and roast them until the thighs move loosely in the joints (about 1 hour).

Serves 4-6

Herbs de Provence

The herbs in this classic mix are not always the same. The ones I like to use are thyme, rosemary, basil, savory and lavender flowers. Others I've seen added are fennel, marjoram and mint. You can find Herbs de Provence in most grocery stores.

If you are in a hurry, you can cut the chicken through the breastbone and lay it flat on a cookie pan. It will reduce the cooking time by about 45 minutes.

1 whole roaster chicken
2 tablespoons Herbs de Provence
1 teaspoon salt
$1/_2$ teaspoon fresh pepper
1 teaspoon paprika
2 tablespoons olive oil

✳ Preheat oven to 400°.
✳ Rub the chicken outside and inside with the herbs, salt, pepper, paprika, and oil.
✳ Bake for $1^1/_2$ hours or until the legs feel loose in the joint.
✳ Serve with mashed potatoes
    Variation:
    Lemon Garlic Chicken
    Follow the instructions above and stuff the chicken with
    one whole lemon cut in half and two heads of garlic. If
    you're roasting it the quick way, place the chicken on top
    of the lemon and garlic, then roast.

Rosemary Chicken And Dumplings

2 to 3 tablespoons olive oil
1 whole chicken, cut into 8 pieces (remove the skin if desired; I usually take the skin off the breast and thighs)
$^1/_4$ cup all-purpose flour
1 teaspoon salt
$^1/_2$ teaspoon fresh black pepper
1 teaspoon paprika
1 large onion, chopped
2 large carrots, chopped
3 stalks celery, chopped
3 cloves minced garlic
1 tablespoon minced fresh parsley
2 tablespoons minced fresh thyme
3 tablespoons minced fresh rosemary
1 cup white wine
2 cups chicken stock

Dumplings:

$^1/_4$ cup shortening
2 cups all-purpose flour
1 teaspoon salt
3 teaspoons baking powder
2 tablespoons minced fresh parsley
$^3/_4$ cup milk

* Heat the oil in a large, wide stockpot over medium-high heat.
* Toss the chicken, flour, salt, pepper and paprika together until the chicken is coated.
* Place the chicken in the heated pot and cook until browned on all sides.
* Add the onions, carrots, celery, garlic, and herbs; cook for another 10-15 minutes until the onions are translucent.
* Add the white wine and stock; bring it to a boil, reduce heat, and simmer, covered, until the meat is tender (about 1 hour).

Dumplings:

* Cut the shortening into the dry ingredients.
* Make a well in the center and stir in the milk.
* Drop 1-inch balls of dough on top of the simmering chicken.
* Cover and cook an additional 10 minutes. NO PEEKING!

Grilled Chicken with Passion Fruit Sauce   *Serves 4*

While down in the Caribbean, I was lucky enough to find some Cornish game hens and was excited about a new recipe I'd created in my head. After preparing a smoked shrimp stuffing they went into the oven. While the hens were cooking, I prepared a pineapple glaze. With 15 minutes of cooking time left, I pulled the hot Pyrex pan out of the oven. Now, if you read the introduction to this book, you know that I didn't pay much attention when it came to cooking at home, and so while professionally trained, I didn't know much about home cooking equipment. The only thing I remembered about Pyrex is that it was unbreakable - or so I thought. I poured the glaze onto the game hens and POP! The whole thing explodes - hot hens, glass and sticky pineapple glaze are all over the counters (what there is of them), cabinets, the sole (floor) and me. And our guests never heard my yelp! Jon and I frantically cleaned the galley while I racked my brain for an elegant entrée I could make in 5 minutes. The Grilled Chicken with Passion Fruit Sauce was the result of that evening's inspired panic.

When I had that Pyrex explosion this is what I made instead. Fast and delicious!

2 whole boneless chicken breasts, split
4 tablespoons olive oil
$^1/_2$ teaspoon salt
$^1/_4$ teaspoon freshly ground black pepper
Juice of two limes

* Combine all of the ingredients in a Ziploc bag or bowl and marinate the chicken breasts for at least half an hour.
* Grill at medium-high heat until the chicken is cooked through, turning at least once.

Passion Fruit Sauce

4 to 6 passion fruit
1 tablespoon honey
Juice of $^1/_2$ lime
$^1/_4$ cup orange juice

* Scoop the insides of the passion fruit into a Cuisinart and add the remaining ingredients.
* Pulse for 1 minute, then strain. Thin with additional orange juice if needed and spoon over the chicken. Serve.

Vegetarian

Caramelized Onion And Gorgonzola Tart

1 teaspoon butter
4 cups thinly sliced onions
1 tablespoon brandy
5 ounces Gorgonzola, crumbled
1 frozen puff pastry sheet
Olive oil as needed
$1/_8$ teaspoon fresh pepper

* Preheat oven to 375°.
* Take the puff pastry out of the freezer to defrost.
* Melt the butter in a large sauté pan over medium heat. Add the onions and cook, stirring frequently, until they are a golden brown color (you may need to turn the heat down so they don't burn). This will take about 20-30 minutes, but the flavor makes it worth the time.
* Just before they are done, add the brandy and cook another minute or two.
* Place the defrosted pastry on an ungreased baking pan and roll the edges over once or twice to create an edge for tart.
* Spread the onions evenly onto the pastry then sprinkle the Gorgonzola and pepperoni top.
* Brush the edges of the pastry with olive oil and bake until the crust is brown and the cheese is melted (about 15 minutes).

3 tablespoons olive oil
3 cloves garlic, mashed and coarsely chopped
1 cup good black or green olives, pitted
2 tablespoons capers
3 anchovies, finely chopped or mashed with the back of a spoon
3 cups peeled and seeded diced tomatoes, or one 28-ounce can diced tomatoes
$^1/_4$ teaspoon freshly ground black pepper
Grated Parmesan cheese and chopped parsley for garnish

✳ Heat the oil in a sauté pan over medium-high heat.
✳ Add garlic and sauté for 30 seconds.
✳ Add the olives, capers and anchovies.
✳ Add the tomatoes and pepper and cook, stirring frequently, about 10 minutes.
✳ Serve over fresh pasta and garnish with the Parmesan and parsley.

Roasted Mushroom and Artichoke Sauce   *Serves 4-6*

1 pound whole clean mushrooms
Olive oil as needed
Salt as needed
Freshly ground black pepper as needed
Artichokes:
2 fresh artichokes
Juice from one lemon
2 tablespoons butter
2 large onions, diced
9 cloves garlic, minced
$1/_2$ teaspoon salt
2 tablespoons all-purpose flour
2 cups chicken stock (or more)
2 cups diced fresh tomatoes, peeled and seeded or one 14-ounce can diced tomatoes
3 tablespoons Marsala wine
2 cups heavy cream
2 teaspoons fresh, minced basil
2 teaspoons fresh, minced thyme
$1/_2$ cup grated Parmesan cheese
$1/_2$ teaspoon salt
Freshly ground black pepper to taste
Grated Parmesan cheese for garnish

* Preheat oven to 450°.
* Place the mushrooms on a roasting pan; and drizzle with olive oil and season with salt and pepper.
* Roast the mushrooms for 15 to 20 minutes.
* Cool and slice the mushrooms. Set aside.
* Trim and cut the artichokes into eighths. Take the choke (that's the fuzzy part) out with a spoon.
* Fill a bowl with water and add the lemon juice and artichokes.
* Heat a large pot on medium-high heat.
* Melt the butter then add the onions, salt and pepper and reduce heat to medium. Cook, stirring frequently, until they are caramelized (20-30 minutes).
* Sprinkle the flour on top of the onions; stir for a minute or so.
* Add the chicken stock and stir vigorously.
* Add the tomatoes, Marsala, cream, herbs and reserved mushrooms and bring to simmer.

✳ Add the cheese and season to taste with salt and pepper.

✳ Add the artichokes and cook until they are done, about 20 minutes.

✳ Serve on top of linguini or fettuccini and garnish with the Parmesan cheese.

"Because Dottie yelled at me"
I've been planning to write this cookbook nearly as long as we've owned the *Riggin*, but building a new yawl boat and sewing quilts for all the passenger berths placed the cookbook somewhat lower on my priority list. Instead, each week I would find myself dictating recipes while passengers eagerly wrote them down. And each week I would tell them there would be a cookbook "someday."

About a year ago I got a slightly firmer nudge to get serious about the cookbook. A repeat passenger of ours, one who comes at least once a year with her husband and who is in marketing, took me firmly by the shoulders, leaned forward (basically in my face) and shouted, "If you made a cookbook, people would buy it!" Since then, I've been saying that I'm doing the cookbook because Dottie yelled at me.

1 large eggplant, peeled and diced
2 tablespoons olive oil
1 large onion, diced
3 cloves garlic, minced
$^1/_2$ teaspoon salt
$^1/_4$ teaspoon freshly ground black pepper
3 cups diced tomatoes, peeled and seeded (or 2 14-ounce cans diced tomatoes)
$^3/_4$ cup red wine
2 tablespoons minced fresh basil
$^1/_2$ cup pine nuts

✻ Place the eggplant in a strainer and lightly sprinkle with salt. Set aside to drain excess liquid for up to an hour.

✻ Heat a large pot over medium heat; and add the olive oil and onions and cook until translucent.

✻ Add the eggplant, garlic, salt and pepper and brown the eggplant.

✻ Add the remaining ingredients except the pine nuts.

✻ Simmer for 30 minutes.

✻ While the sauce is simmering place the pine nuts in a sauté pan and roast them over medium heat until they are golden brown, stirring often. This takes about 5 minutes.

✻ When you are ready to serve, either stir in the pine nuts or sprinkle them on top.

✻ Serve with your favorite pasta.

Summer Vegetable Strata

12 slices of day old or dry French or Italian Bread, cut in $^1/_2$ inch slices
1 clove garlic, slightly crushed
5 large eggs
2 cups milk
$^1/_2$ cup freshly grated Parmesan cheese
$^1/_2$ teaspoon salt
$^1/_4$ teaspoon pepper
1 cup loosely packed fresh chopped basil leaves
2 tablespoons olive oil
1 small onion, finely chopped
2 medium summer squash or zucchini, washed and cut into quarters
lengthwise, then cut into pieces about $^1/_2$-inch thick
2 tomatoes, seeded and roughly chopped

✳ Preheat oven to 350°. Lightly butter a 9 x 13-inch baking dish.
✳ Rub the top of each slice of bread with the garlic clove.
✳ Lay the slices in the dish in one layer, cutting them into pieces when necessary.
✳ Season lightly with salt and pepper.
✳ In a separate bowl, whisk the eggs then whisk in the milk, half of the cheese, and a generous amount of salt and pepper.
✳ Add the basil and stir gently. Set aside.
✳ Heat the oil in a large sauté pan over medium-high heat. Add the onion, and cook, stirring occasionally, until it softens and colors lightly.
✳ Stir the squash into the onion, spread everything in a single layer, and let it sit undisturbed for 1 to 2 minutes to encourage browning; turn and continue cooking another 1 to 2 minutes until browned.
✳ When the squash is lightly browned on both sides, stir in the tomatoes, stir to toss, and remove from heat.
✳ Use a slotted spoon to drain off any excess liquid and spread the vegetables evenly over the bread.
✳ Give the milk and egg mixture a stir and gently pour it all into the dish.
✳ Top with the remaining cheese.
✳ Bake until the milk and egg mixture sets, about 40-45 minutes.
✳ Cool at least 5 minutes, cut into squares and serve.

Tomato, Leek And Brie with Linguini *Serves 2*

1 tablespoon butter
1 clove garlic, minced
1 large leek, cut in half lengthwise, thoroughly washed, and thinly sliced
2 ripe tomatoes, peeled, seeded, and diced
3 tablespoons white wine
4 ounces brie
Salt and pepper to taste

✳ Prepare enough linguini for two while making the sauce.
✳ Melt the butter in a sauté pan over medium heat.
✳ Add the garlic and sauté it briefly.
✳ Add the leeks and cook until tender.
✳ Add the tomatoes and wine; bring the sauce to a simmer, then whisk in the brie a few pieces at a time.
✳ When the brie is melted, season to taste with salt and pepper, toss with the linguini and serve.

Tomato, Mascarpone and Kalamata Olive Pasta *Serves 4*

1 tablespoon extra-virgin olive oil
4 cloves fresh garlic, minced
4 to 5 large plum tomatoes, peeled, seeded, and diced
32 black Kalamata olives, pitted
8 ounces Mascarpone cheese
2 tablespoons white wine
Salt and fresh black pepper to taste
Garnish:
1 cup freshly grated Parmesan cheese
$^{1}/_{4}$ cup chopped fresh parsley

* Prepare enough pasta for four while making the sauce.
* Heat a sauté pan over medium heat. Add the olive oil and garlic and sauté for about 30 seconds.
* Add the tomatoes and toss lightly; add the olives and cook for an additional minute or so.
* Add the wine and Mascarpone and cook until the cheese is melted. This whole process should not take long at all, maybe one minute. The point is not to stew the tomatoes, but have them retain their fresh taste.
* Season to taste with salt and pepper.
* Arrange the pasta on the plates, sprinkle the Parmesan cheese it, then spoon the sauce on top of the cheese. Garnish with the parsley. Mangia!

Yeast Breads

The scent of baking bread and wood smoke is a guaranteed way to get our mouths watering. All of the recipes here include directions for making bread by hand and by machine. While I would always champion hand-kneaded, hand-shaped, woodstove or oven-baked bread, I would also choose homemade over store-bought any day. If a machine gets you homemade, healthy bread rather than bread filled with preservatives so it will last for weeks, then so be it. There's more to bread than just the production of it. It's the smell, the care, the warmth of bread made at home that makes a difference.

It's true that flavor is sacrificed when using a bread machine; but it's also true that I won't make bread as often at home if I'm not using the bread machine. I've provided instructions for making bread in a machine because we are all busy and I still want you to be able to use these recipes. That's what they are here for - to be used! I've tested each recipe in a Zojirushi and listed the ingredients in the order that they should be added according to my machine. Some machines require you to add ingredients in a different order; if so then follow that order instead of the order in the recipes.

There are a couple of things I focus on each time I make yeast bread by hand. Each enhances the flavor and texture of the bread.

Kneading

There is no way that you can over-knead a loaf of bread by hand. Be more cautious, however, if you are using a dough hook. Usually my mess cooks are asking "Am I done yet?" long before the bread is fully kneaded. The most important result of kneading is the development of gluten, which keeps the bread from falling. You want to vigorously knead the dough for at least 10 minutes.

Rising

The longer it takes the dough to rise, the more flavor and texture it will have. You can even put dough in the refrigerator to rise overnight.

Proofing

I don't proof my yeast (see if it's active) every time I use it. But if you need to dust the top of the yeast container before using it, then you should proof the yeast. Just place the required yeast in half of the warm water and wait 5 minutes. If it bubbles, it's active. Also be sure to stir the flour, salt and yeast briefly stirred first, then add the remaining ingredients. This insures that the salt and yeast don't end up in clumps.

Flour vs. Water

When making bread it's better to use a fixed amount of flour and then add water to adjust the texture of the dough (rather than add additional flour after you've mixed everything together). Adding more flour changes the ratio of all the other ingredients to the flour, and therefore changes the flavor. Water doesn't add or subtract any flavor. I do use flour to dust the counter top when I'm kneading, but I make sure that I don't need to add a whole cup of flour to get the dough to not be sticky. Better to have not added so much water.

Steam

I always make sure to create steam in my oven whenever I'm baking bread; the loaf rises higher and has a crisper, thicker crust. There are two ways that I've found that work to create steam in a home oven. The best method is to always have a skillet filled with rocks on the floor of the oven. Tossing a cup of water in the skillet generates more steam – like a sauna – and keeps it contained. Failing this, 3-4 cubes of ice thrown in a pan on the oven floor works too.

Flour

I'm a King Arthur flour fan. We use 50 pounds of it per week! If you can't get it in your area, see the **Local Sources** list near the back of the book for contact info.

Anadama Bread

Makes 3 loaves

1¼ cups corn meal
4½ cups boiling water
3 tablespoons yeast
1½ tablespoons salt
¾ cup warm water
4½ cups all-purpose flour
4½ cups whole wheat flour
1 cup molasses
⅓ cup vegetable oil or butter

✳ Pour the boiling water over the corn meal. Cool until lukewarm.

✳ Combine the yeast, salt, and flours in a separate bowl.

✳ Stir in all the remaining ingredients (including the cornmeal mixture). Add more water if needed.

✳ Knead for 10-15 minutes.

✳ Oil the bowl and the top of the dough, cover, and place in a warm place to rise for 30-45 minutes, until doubled.

✳ Preheat oven to 375°. Grease 3 loaf pans and sprinkle them with cornmeal.

✳ Punch down the dough, form three loaves and place them in the loaf pans. Cover and allow to rise again.

✳ Place the pans in the oven, throw a cup of water over hot stones set in a pan in the bottom of the oven (or toss 3 to 4 ice cubes into a pan in the bottom of the oven) to generate steam and **quickly** close the oven door. Bake until a deep brown (about 45 minutes).

For bread machine: Makes one 2-pound loaf

½ cup corn meal
1¾ cups boiling water
2¾ cups **bread** flour
1½ cups whole wheat flour
⅓ cup molasses
1 tablespoon yeast
1½ teaspoons salt
2 tablespoons butter

Add the ingredients in the order listed above or in the order required for your machine. Some machines require that the flour go in first. You must use bread flour rather than all-purpose flour. It's not necessary for the corn meal and boiling water mixture to cool before adding all the other ingredients, as it is not in direct contact with the yeast. If, however, your bread machine requires that the dry ingredients go in first then you must cool the corn meal and water mixture before adding it.

Crusty Peasant Bread

For bread machine: Makes
one 2-pound loaf

1¾ cups water
5 cups **bread** flour
2 teaspoons salt
1 tablespoon olive oil
2 teaspoons yeast

¨Add the ingredients in the
order listed above or in the
order required for your
machine. Some machines
require that the flour go in
first. You must use bread
flour rather than all-
purpose flour.

$1^1/_2$ tablespoons dry yeast
1 tablespoon salt
5 cups all-purpose flour
2 cups warm water
2 tablespoons olive oil
Cornmeal for dusting

✳ Combine the yeast, salt, and flour in a large bowl.
✳ Stir in all the remaining ingredients, reserving   cup water. Add more
 water if needed.
✳ Knead for 10-15 minutes.
✳ Oil the bowl and the top of the dough, cover, and set aside in a warm,
 draft free place to rise until doubled (about 1 hour).
✳ Preheat oven to 350°.
✳ Divide the dough into the number of loaves you plan to make; shape them
 into long French-style loaves.
✳ Dust a cookie pan with corn meal and place the loaves onto the pan.
 Cover and allow to rise again.
✳ When the loaves have nearly doubled, make three diagonal slashes on each
 loaf with a razor or very sharp knife.
✳ Place the pans in the oven, throw a cup of water over hot stones set in a
 pan in the bottom of the oven (or toss 3 to 4 ice cubes into a pan in the
 bottom of the oven) to generate steam and **quickly** close the oven door.
✳ Bake until golden brown (around 30-45 minutes depending on the size of
 the loaves).

Focaccia

We usually have focaccia at some point during the week. I make it with several of the toppings, below, for lunch, or as an accompaniment to an entrée. It's the same recipe as the Crusty Peasant Bread, used a different way.

$1^1/_2$ tablespoons dry yeast
1 tablespoon salt
5 cups all-purpose flour
2 cups warm water
2 tablespoons olive oil
Cornmeal for dusting

✳ Combine the yeast, salt, and flour in a large bowl.

✳ Stir in all the remaining ingredients, reserving $^1/_4$ cup water. Add more water if needed.

✳ Knead for 10-15 minutes.

✳ Oil the bowl and the top of the dough, cover, and set aside in a warm, draft free place to rise until doubled (about 1 hour).

✳ Preheat oven to 350° and oil two cookie pans.

✳ After the first rise divide the dough and place half on each pan. Work both pieces flat either with your hands or with a rolling pin. If the dough is fighting you (keeps shrinking back when you stretch it), just let it rest for 5 minutes and continue until it reaches the edge of the cookie pan.

✳ Oil the top of the dough and let it rise until doubled. Press your fingers quickly into the dough all over the surface as if you were playing the piano and then dust with both salt and pepper. Bake until golden brown (around 35 minutes).

Some of my favorite focaccia toppings:
Green Olive Tapenade and goat cheese
Ricotta and Prosciutto
Caramelized Onion, Sautéed Green and Red Peppers with Onion
Red Onion, Mushroom and Parmesan Cheese

Stovetop Focaccia

Our good friend Jim Amaral is a baker and owns a fabulous statewide bakery called Borealis Breads. He uses organic local wheat and has done more for the quality of bread making in the state than any other business around. He and his family came sailing with us a few years ago and when he saw my woodstove, his first comment was how great it would be to bake flat bread on TOP of the stove. After several tries and the indignity of having smoke billowing from my galley, I now make stovetop focaccia at least once a week. I clean the stovetop and throw a fairly thin piece of dough directly on the stove surface. I need to move it frequently as there are many hot spots that will scorch the bread. Once I've flipped the bread over, I oil it, sprinkle it with salt and pepper, and serve immediately.

Jiffy Oatmeal Bread

Makes 2 loaves

$1^1/_2$ cups boiling water
1 cup quick oatmeal
2 tablespoons dry yeast
$5^1/_2$ cups all-purpose flour, sifted
4 teaspoons salt
$^1/_2$ cup molasses
$^1/_3$ cup cooking oil
$1^1/_2$ cups evaporated milk
1 egg

✳ Mix the boiling water and oatmeal together in a large bowl and set aside to cool.
✳ Mix the dry ingredients in a separate bowl, then stir in the oatmeal and all the remaining ingredients, reserving $^1/_4$ cup water. Mix thoroughly and add the reserved water if needed.
✳ Knead for 10-15 minutes.
✳ Oil the bowl and the top of the dough, cover, and set aside in a warm draft free place to rise until doubled.
✳ Preheat oven to 350°.
✳ Cut the dough into 2 equal pieces and let it rest, covered, for 5 minutes.
✳ Shape the dough into loaves and put them on an ungreased cookie pan. Cover and allow to rise again.
✳ When the loaves have nearly doubled, slash the tops with a razor or very sharp knife.
✳ Place the pans in the oven, throw a cup of water over hot stones set in a pan in the bottom of the oven (or toss 3 to 4 ice cubes into a pan in the bottom of the oven) to generate steam and **quickly** close the oven door. Bake until golden brown (around 45 minutes).

Jim's Raisin Bread

Makes 2 loaves

Jim is a true Maine character; I've known him ever since I started working on the windjammers. He's panned for gold in the Camden Hills, taught me how to upholster my first chair, and done just about everything else in between. He gave me this recipe – it's easy, delicious and it always works.

8 cups all-purpose flour
2 packages (2 tablespoons) yeast
1 tablespoon salt
$3^1/_2$ cups warm water
$^1/_2$ cup cooking oil
$^1/_3$ cup sugar
2 cups raisins
1 egg (optional)

* Combine the dry ingredients in a large bowl.
* Stir in all the remaining ingredients, reserving $^1/_4$ cup water. Add more water if needed.
* Knead for 10-15 minutes.
* Oil the bowl and the top of the dough, cover, and set aside in a warm, draft free place to rise until doubled (about 1 hour).
* Preheat oven to 350°.
* Divide the dough in half; shape them into long French-style loaves.
* Dust a cookie pan with corn meal and place the loaves onto the pan. Cover and allow to rise again.
* When the loaves have nearly doubled, make three diagonal slashes on each loaf with a razor or very sharp knife.
* Place the pans in the oven, throw a cup of water over hot stones set in a pan in the bottom of the oven (or toss 3 to 4 ice cubes into a pan in the bottom of the oven) to generate steam and **quickly** close the oven door. Bake until golden brown (around 35-40 minutes).

For bread machine:Makes one 2-pound loaf

4 cups bread flour
1 tablespoon yeast
1½ teaspoons salt
1¾ cups warm water
4 tablespoons cooking oil
2 tablespoons sugar
1 cup raisins

Add the ingredients in the order listed above or in the order required for your machine. Some machines require that the flour go in first. You must use bread flour rather than all-purpose flour.

Newfi Bread

Makes 3 loaves

For bread machine: Makes one 2-pound loaf

1½ cups water
*4½ cups **bread** flour*
1 tablespoon butter
½ cup molasses
1½ teaspoons salt
2 teaspoons yeast

Add the ingredients in the order listed above or in the order required for your machine. Some machines require that the flour go in first. You must use bread flour rather than all-purpose flour.

This recipe is a favorite on many vessels in the windjammer fleet.

2 tablespoons (2 packages) dry yeast
$^1/_2$ tablespoon salt
8 cups white all-purpose flour
3 cups warm water
2 tablespoons soft butter
1 cup molasses

✳ Pour the boiling water over the corn meal. Cool until lukewarm.
✳ Combine the yeast, salt, and flour in a large bowl.
✳ Stir in all the remaining ingredients, reserving $^1/_4$ cup water. Add more water if needed.
✳ Knead for 10-15 minutes.
✳ Oil the bowl and the top of the dough, cover, and place in a warm place to rise for 30-45 minutes, until doubled.
✳ Preheat oven to 375°. Grease 3 loaf pans.
✳ Punch down the dough, form three loaves and place them in the loaf pans. Cover and allow to rise again until nearly doubled.
✳ Place the pans in the oven, throw a cup of water over hot stones set in a pan in the bottom of the oven (or toss 3 to 4 ice cubes into a pan in the bottom of the oven) to generate steam and **quickly** close the oven door. Bake until deep brown (around 45 minutes).

Sunflower Millet Bread

Makes 2 loaves

For bread machine:Makes one 2-pound loaf.

$1^1/_2$ cups water
1 cup raw millet
$2^1/_2$ teaspoons salt
$^1/_4$ cup ($^1/_2$ stick) butter
3 tablespoons honey
2 packages dry yeast
3 cups unbleached white all-purpose flour
3 cups whole wheat flour
1 cup sunflower seeds, unsalted
1 cup lukewarm water

* Bring the water to a boil and add the millet, salt, butter and honey.
* Reduce heat and simmer until all the water is absorbed (around 15 minutes).
* Remove from heat; cool until lukewarm.
* Combine all the dry ingredients in a large bowl.
* Stir in the millet mixture and $^1/_4$ cup of water. Add more water if needed.
* Knead for 10-15 minutes.
* Oil the bowl and the top of the dough, cover, and set aside in a warm, draft free place to rise until doubled (about 1 hour).
* Preheat oven to 350°.
* Divide the dough in half; shape them into long French-style loaves.
* Dust a cookie pan with corn meal and place the loaves onto the pan. Cover and allow to rise again.
* When the loaves have nearly doubled, make three diagonal slashes on each loaf with a razor or very sharp knife.
* Place the pans in the oven, throw a cup of water over hot stones set in a pan in the bottom of the oven (or toss 3 to 4 ice cubes into a pan in the bottom of the oven) to generate steam and **quickly** close the oven door.
* Bake until golden brown, about 45 minutes.

¾ cup water
½ cup raw millet
1¼ teaspoons salt
2 tablespoons butter
1½ tablespoons honey
1 cup lukewarm water
1½ cups unbleached bread flour
1½ cups whole wheat flour
½ cup sunflower seeds, unsalted
1 package dry yeast
1 tablespoon vital wheat gluten

Bring the water to a boil; add the millet, salt, butter and honey. Cook until all the water is absorbed (about 15 minutes). Remove from heat and cool until lukewarm. Spoon the cooled millet mixture into the bread machine. Add the remaining ingredients in the order listed above or in the order required for your machine.

Very Easy Bread Recipe

This is one the kids make at school. The girls and I make it at home as well.

1$^1/_2$ tablespoon dry yeast
1 cup warm water
1 stick ($^1/_2$ cup) butter, softened
5 tablespoons of honey
1 tablespoon salt
3 cups warm milk
4 to 5 cups whole wheat flour, sifted
4 to 5 cups all-purpose flour, sifted

✳ Mix the yeast, water, butter, honey, salt and milk in a large bowl.
✳ Stir in the sifted flour and mix it in with a wooden spoon. You can add other secret ingredients, like raisins, oats, cinnamon, rye and/or nuts.
✳ Cover and set in a warm place to rise 10 to 15 minutes.
✳ Preheat oven to 350°. Oil two cookie pans.
✳ Turn the dough out onto a floured surface and knead for 5-10 minutes.
✳ When the dough becomes very smooth and elastic form it into rolls.
✳ Place the rolls on the prepared cookie pans. If you have time you can let them rise again, covered, on the cookie pan.
✳ Bake the rolls until they are light brown, about 20 minutes.

Rhyme to try while kneading the dough...
This is the way we push the dough,
Push the dough, push the dough.
This is the way we push the dough,
So early in the morning!

Whole Wheat Walnut Bread   *Makes 2 loaves*

3 cups whole wheat flour
3 cups all-purpose flour
1 tablespoon (1 package) dry yeast
1 tablespoon packed brown sugar
2 tablespoons molasses
2 tablespoons melted margarine or butter
1 tablespoon salt
$^1/_3$ cup dry milk
$2^1/_4$ cups warm water
1 cup whole walnuts

✳ Combine both flours and the yeast in a large bowl.
✳ Stir in all the remaining ingredients, reserving $^1/_4$ cup water. Add more water if needed.
✳ Knead for 10-15 minutes.
✳ Oil the bowl and the top of the dough, cover, and set aside in a warm, draft free place to rise until doubled (about 1 hour).
✳ Preheat oven to 350°.
✳ Divide the dough in half; shape them into 2 round loaves.
✳ Place the loaves on a cookie pan. Cover and allow to rise again.
✳ When the loaves have nearly doubled, make three diagonal slashes on each loaf with a razor or very sharp knife.
✳ Place the pans in the oven, throw a cup of water over hot stones set in a pan in the bottom of the oven (or toss 3 to 4 ice cubes into a pan in the bottom of the oven) to generate steam and **quickly** close the oven door. Bake until golden brown (around 35 minutes).

For bread machine:Makes one 2-pound loaf

1¾ cups water
2 cups whole wheat flour
2½ cups bread flour
2 teaspoons yeast
1½ teaspoons salt
$^1/_3$ cup dried milk
1 tablespoon vital wheat gluten
2 tablespoons butter
2 tablespoons molasses
$^3/_4$ cup whole walnuts

Add the ingredients in the order listed above or in the order required for your machine. Some machines require that the flour go in first. You must use bread flour rather than all-purpose flour.

Biscuits, Quick Breads and Muffins

Due to time, space, and other constraints while cooking onboard, I've ruthlessly streamlined the process for making biscuits, quick breads, and muffins.

A lot of true bakers, which I will admit I am not, will tell you that you need to use 15 bowls to make a few simple muffins. One for the pre-sifted, pre-measured flour, one for the creamed ingredients, one for a finger bowl.... Not me. On the boat and at home we have limited resources in water, energy and/or time and (I know you can appreciate this) we want as few dirty dishes as possible. With that in mind, the way I mix my ingredients depends on what type of ingredients they are. I break the ingredients down into three groups: creamed, dry and liquid.

If there is creaming to be done, it gets done first; butter and sugar creamed in a big bowl, then eggs and sometimes a few other ingredients. The dry ingredients all go into the sifter, with a plate or something underneath it to catch what comes out the bottom. The dry ingredients get sifted into the bowl with the creamed ingredients, and then I add any additional liquid and mix it all up. One bowl, no lumps.

If there is no creaming to be done, then the dry ingredients get sifted into a large bowl. I make a well in the center where all of the wet ingredients go. The eggs go first and I scramble them in the well. Then the rest of the wet ingredients go in and I start mixing the dry ingredients in from the center and work out. Again, one bowl, no lumps.

The dry ingredients don't get sifted beforehand - too many dishes. I've made whatever adjustments need to be made to reduce the amount of flour so the recipes come out properly. The one thing I stick to religiously is to level off my measuring cups and spoons with a knife or anything flat. This makes a big difference in the final product and also in my ability to make the taste and texture consistent every time I make it.

Out of Buttermilk?

The recipes I have from my grandma all have buttermilk in them. On the boat, to simplify shopping, I buy one kind of milk – whole milk. When I need buttermilk for a recipe, I add 1 to 2 tablespoons of lemon juice or cider vinegar to a little less than 1 cup of milk.

This is a recipe my grandma passed on to me through my mom; it's great because it's so versatile. I can make the biscuits according to the recipe below, or I can add to it to make cheddar cheese, lemon and herb, Parmesan and black pepper, or Roquefort and walnut biscuits. I've listed all these variations in the pages that follow. I also alter this recipe slightly to make scones (page 157).

2 cups all-purpose flour, sifted
2 teaspoons baking powder
$^1/_2$ teaspoon salt
$^1/_4$ cup shortening
$^3/_4$ cup milk

✳ Preheat oven to 450°.
✳ Sift together the flour, baking powder, and salt. This is an important step because you want to add air to the mixture so the biscuits are as fluffy as possible.
✳ Cut the shortening in with a pastry knife (or your fingers) until the mixture is the texture of coarse meal. Stir in any additional dry ingredients here (cheese, pepper, etc.).
✳ Add milk and any additional wet ingredients, stirring until a soft dough forms.
✳ *Do not overmix.* This is very important; if you overmix you will probably get hard tack instead of fluffy biscuits.
✳ Turn out onto a floured board and knead 10 times, then STOP!
✳ Roll or pat out the dough until it is $^1/_2$-inch thick. Cut with a floured 2-inch biscuit cutter.
✳ Bake on ungreased cookie pan for 12 to 15 minutes.

Variations:
Lemon and Herb Biscuits
To the basic recipe add:
Zest from one lemon
1 teaspoon lemon juice
3 tablespoons of fresh herbs such as chives and/or chive blossoms, lemon thyme, thyme, rosemary, lavender

Parmesan and Black Pepper Biscuits
To the basic recipe add:
2 teaspoons fresh black pepper
Parmesan and Black Pepper Biscuits
To the basic recipe add:

2 teaspoons fresh black pepper
$^1/_2$ teaspoon baking soda
1 cup grated Parmesan cheese
1 egg, beaten
A little extra milk if needed

Roquefort and Walnut Biscuits
To the basic recipe add:
$^1/_4$ lb crumbled Roquefort
$^1/_2$ cup finely chopped walnuts or pecans
$^1/_8$ teaspoon cayenne
1 pinch paprika
1 egg yolk
2 tablespoons heavy cream

2 cups all-purpose flour
1 tablespoon sugar
$2^1/_2$ teaspoons baking powder
$^1/_2$ teaspoon ground black pepper
$^1/_2$ teaspoon baking soda
$^1/_2$ teaspoon salt
6 tablespoons chilled unsalted butter, cut into $^1/_2$-inch pieces
$1^1/_4$ cups grated extra-sharp cheddar cheese
$^3/_4$ to 1 cup cold buttermilk
1 large egg, beaten
1 tablespoon milk
Poppy seeds for garnish

* Preheat oven to 400°.
* Combine the first six ingredients in a large mixing bowl.
* Use a pastry cutter or your hands to cut the butter into the mixture until it resembles a fine meal.
* Stir in the cheese.
* Mix the buttermilk into flour mixture just until the dough binds together.
* Turn out onto a floured surface and knead gently until combined, about 10 turns. Pat the dough out to a $^3/_4$-inch thickness.
* Cut into biscuits with a 2-inch cookie cutter.
* Transfer the biscuits to an ungreased cookie pan.
* Whisk together the egg and milk and brush over the biscuits with a pastry brush; sprinkle with poppy seeds.
* Bake until golden brown and firm to touch, about 13 minutes.

Scones

2 cups sifted all-purpose flour
2 teaspoons baking powder
$^1/_4$ cup sugar
$^1/_2$ teaspoon salt
6 tablespoons cold butter
$^1/_2$ cup raisins
$^3/_4$ cup milk
1 egg

* Preheat oven to 450°.
* Sift together the flour, baking powder, sugar and salt. This is an important step because you want to add air to the mixture so the scones are as light as possible.
* Cut the shortening in with a pastry knife (or your fingers) until the mixture is the texture of coarse meal. Stir in any additional dry ingredients here (raisins, nuts, etc.).
* Add the milk, egg and any additional wet ingredients, stirring until a soft dough forms.
* *Do not overmix.* This is very important; if you overmix you will probably get hard tack instead of scones.
* Turn out onto a floured board and knead 10 times, then STOP!
* Roll or pat the dough until it is $^1/_2$-inch thick. Cut with a floured $1^1/_2$-inch biscuit cutter.
* Bake on ungreased cookie pan for 12 to 15 minutes.

To make one large scone:
Place the dough on a cookie pan and shape it into a circle about 6 to 7 inches in diameter.
Brush the top with a tiny bit of half and half and sprinkle with sugar.
Score the "pie" into 8 to 10 pieces.
Increase the baking time to 15-20 minutes.

Variations
Replace raisins with:
Chopped crystallized ginger
Chopped almonds, walnuts or pecans
Any dried fruit such as blueberries, cherries, craisins, apricots

My favorite combinations are:

Apricot and Almond
Dried Cherries and Walnuts
Crystallized Ginger and Apricot

Blueberry Lemon Bread

$1^1/_2$ cups all-purpose flour
1 teaspoon baking powder
$1/_4$ cup salt
6 tablespoons unsalted butter
1 cup sugar
2 large eggs
2 teaspoons freshly grated lemon peel
$1/_2$ cup milk
$1^1/_2$ cups fresh blueberries

Glaze

3 tablespoons fresh lemon juice
$1/_3$ cup sugar

✳ Preheat oven to 325°. Grease one loaf pan.
✳ Combine the flour, baking powder, and salt. Set aside.
✳ In a large mixing bowl, cream the butter with 1 cup sugar.
✳ Add eggs one at a time, mixing well each time.
✳ Add the lemon peel.
✳ Mix the dry ingredients, alternating with the milk (about one third at a time), into the sugar/egg mixture. Be sure to add the dry ingredients last.
✳ Fold in the blueberries and spoon into the pan.
✳ Bake 1 hour 15 minutes, until the bread springs back when lightly pressed in the center. Leave in the pan.
✳ When the bread is out of the oven bring the glaze ingredients to a boil, stirring until the sugar dissolves.
✳ Pierce the top of the hot loaf several times with a toothpick and pour the lemon mixture over the loaf.
✳ Cool completely, and remove from the pan.

Blueberry Muffins

I use this recipe as a base for many different kinds of muffins. It's very forgiving and tasty too.

>2 cups all-purpose flour
>$^2/_3$ cup sugar
>1 tablespoon baking powder
>$^3/_4$ teaspoon salt
>$^1/_3$ cup vegetable oil
>2 large eggs, beaten
>$^2/_3$ cups milk
>$1^1/_3$ cups blueberries

* Preheat oven to 350°.
* Grease (or line with muffin papers) muffin pans.
* Sift together dry ingredients.
* Add oil, egg, and milk. Stir until just mixed.
* Gently fold in the blueberries; then fill the muffin cups two-thirds full.
* Bake for 20 minutes, until the muffins spring back when lightly pressed in the center.

I also make pumpkin, honey and walnut muffins with this recipe. Reduce the milk to $^1/_3$ cup; add 2 tablespoons honey and 1 cup canned or fresh cooked pumpkin with the other liquid ingredients, then stir in $^3/_4$ cup chopped walnuts instead of the blueberries.

Other favorite variations: replace the blueberries with
Dried cranberries
Raisins
Dried apricots
Chocolate chips

Applesauce Muffins

2 cups all-purpose flour
1 tablespoon baking powder
$^1/_2$ cup brown sugar
$^1/_2$ teaspoon baking soda
$^1/_2$ teaspoon salt
$^1/_2$ teaspoon cinnamon
$^1/_2$ teaspoon nutmeg
$^1/_2$ cup raisins
$^1/_4$ cup ($^1/_2$ stick) butter
1 cup applesauce
$^1/_4$ cup milk
1 large egg

* Preheat oven to 425° and grease muffin pans.
* Combine the dry ingredients and raisins together in a mixing bowl.
* Melt the butter in a small saucepan; cool slightly, then whisk in the applesauce, egg, and milk.
* Stir the applesauce mixture into the dry ingredients until just blended.
* Fill the greased muffin cups two-thirds full with the batter.
* Bake 15-20 minutes.

A Week at Sea

Sunday:

It's just before boarding on Sunday night; the crew does a few last minute touches of polish on the brass, one more check of the deck to make sure all the lines are flemished and coiled, and at 5 pm the first guests start to arrive. We greet them warmly – some are first-time passengers, some are repeat passengers who return every year. One returning couple tells us that their trip on the *Riggin* starts when they get in the car to leave their house; off comes the watch and it doesn't go back on until they hit the dock after a week onboard.

Everyone stows their gear in their cabins, then are shown around the deck and galley by one of our crew. They pause to help themselves to hot coffee or tea and homemade cookies, then start meeting their fellow passengers and crew. I'm meeting passengers as I arrange the flowers I've just brought over from the garden behind our house. A harbor seal pops his head up and eyes us curiously.

At 6 pm Captain Jon gathers everyone 'round for "captain's call" – introducing them to the ins and outs of shipboard living and talking about what to expect for the week. Except for the hottest days of the summer, the wood stove is a welcome source of heat in the evening as the air cools; folks gather in the varnished pine galley to read or get to know each other.

Monday:

Too excited to sleep, most everyone's up early Monday morning. The crew is bucketing down the decks, packing ice and loading wood. A week's worth of provisions is carefully loaded and packed in ice, arranged in the order of when they will be used. I've been up since 4:30; coffee is ready and on deck by 7 am. After a hearty breakfast of pancakes and bacon, passengers go ashore for any last minute items they've forgotten – foul weather gear, extra film and batteries for their cameras, soda, wine and beer.

Breakfast is over and cleaned up. Some folks, already eager to help, work with the crew to take down the awning and prepare the *Riggin* for departure. Finally it's time. We cast off lines, everyone helps to raise the sails, and we're off. The moment that the sails are raised and the yawl boat engine is turned off there seems to be a collective sigh – of relief, happiness, peace. A favorite place on the boat once the sails are up is at the bow; one passenger of ours can always be found there at this time "clearing my head." There's a joy to being back out on the bay – our motto at this point is, "If we don't have it, we don't need it."

We aren't alone – other windjammers are leaving their homeport as well. It's a majestic sight. As we pass both the Rockland and Owl's Head Lighthouses and look south across the sparkling water, all we can see is open space – sky and water. To the north and west are the legendary Camden Hills and all of the splendid islands of Penobscot Bay. The breeze is brisk so we have time to play. As we race up to Camden to see the boats entering the bay, we're feeling the wind on our cheeks, the exciting motion of the schooner, and the sound of the waves lapping against the bow.

After a magical first day, we ghost into Buck's Harbor. A talented steel band frequently performs by the general store and tonight is no exception. After dinner we all go ashore to explore, walk around and listen to the music. Robert McCloskey wrote about Bucks Harbor in his renowned children's book *One Morning in Maine*. He was a two-time Caldecott Medalist – *Make Way for Ducklings* won in 1942 and *Time of Wonder* in 1958. He also wrote *Blueberries for Sal*, our family's favorite.

Monday Menu

Breakfast – Maine Blueberry Pancakes, Maine maple syrup, butcher's cut bacon, assorted melon wedges, fresh juice

Lunch – Curried Lamb and Lentil Stew, garden salad with nasturtiums, Dana's Maple-Dill Dressing, sunflower seeds, feta cheese, Mom's Brown Bread, Ginger Shortbread

Appetizer – Warm Cheddar and Horseradish Dip in Bread Bowls

Dinner – Poached Salmon with Tri-Pepper Salsa, basmati rice, green peas with mushrooms, Whole Wheat Walnut bread, Strawberry Shortcake

Tuesday:

It's a sunny morning and this is the warmest harbor we will be in all week long. My girls know it – so they talk me into going swimming with them. This convinces a few sturdy folks to give it a try also. Some are in and out – you almost wonder if they got wet! Others discover that it's refreshing and stay in to swim around the boat and maybe wash their hair (we have a shower onboard but many passengers still prefer to wash their hair with fresh seawater). While we are swimming, the crew is busy readying the boat for sail. This is the first morning we raise the anchor – it's all done by hand and is a real team effort! What satisfaction to sail off the anchor under our own power and through the efforts of those on board.

It's one of those meandering days so we turn southwest to head down Eggemoggin Reach. There is a high suspension bridge that connects Little Deer Island to the mainland. We sail under it calling "ollie, ollie oxen free!" Once, we saw three deer here — swimming from the mainland to Little Deer Island. Folks settle in fairly quickly today, finding a favorite spot on a cabin top for reading, or on the bowsprit quietly looking out to sea. Many are on the quarterdeck by the wheel, listening to Captain Jon answer questions and tell a few stories.

After a leisurely day we find ourselves anchored in Burnt Coat Harbor on Swan's Island, a snug and pretty harbor that boasts an historic lighthouse and residents that can trace their family roots back to the Boston Tea Party. Jon pulls out his guitar

and soon we're singing favorite songs of the sea, and of the ships and people that make the ocean their home.

Tuesday Menu

Breakfast – Toasted Oatmeal, Granola, milk, brown sugar, raisins, Warm Fruit Compote, Sue's Breakfast Muffins

Lunch – Clam Chowder, Lemon and Chive Biscuits, Garbanzo Bean and Roasted Eggplant Salad, pickles, oyster crackers, Almond Poppy Seed Cake

Appetizer – Raspberry Dip with apples and pears

Dinner – New England Boiled Dinner (corned beef, turnips, carrots, potatoes, cabbage, and onions) Mustard Sauce, Irish Soda Bread, Apple Crisp

Wednesday:

Wanting to explore a bit, several of us go ashore and walk out to Burnt Coat Harbor Light on Hockamock Head, admiring wildflowers and seashells on our route. We take pictures and leave the wildflowers and seashells for others to appreciate as well. Singing to raise the sails, the cadence is easy to adopt and the sails go up quickly. I am in our yawl boat *Pearl* pushing the schooner out of the harbor. Jon built her a few winters back out of local oak, cedar, brown heart and silver baly. She is our tugboat and our launch; she helps us get where we need to go when we don't have enough wind and ferries us ashore for walks and shopping.

Wednesdays are one of my favorite days of the week. It's on this day that shoulders relax, laughter is easy, conversations meaningful, and even moments of silence are noted and appreciated. There is a simpler appreciation of our surroundings. This day is the turning point as the magic and the slower tempo of being on Penobscot Bay really seeps in and the hectic pace of our lives on shore falls away.

By late afternoon we've dropped the "hook" (anchor) in Stonington. Lobster boats cluster around the harbor and houses seem to protect the hill. This is a true lobstering village. From the deck we can see one building painted with huge letters, spelling out "Opera House". It's nearly time for dinner; but there'll be plenty of time to go ashore tomorrow. After smelling dinner all afternoon long, we finally get a taste. All hands sit in a galley made cozy by the light of kerosene lanterns and fresh flowers on the table.

Wednesday Menu

Breakfast - Scrambled eggs, locally made sausage, Baking Powder Biscuits, grapefruit wedges, homemade Strawberry Jam and butter

Lunch – Zucchini and Genoa Salami Deep-Dish Pizza, garden salad, Creamy Herb Dressing, Congo Bars

Appetizer – Roasted Red Pepper and Artichoke Dip with tortilla chips

Dinner – Fettuccini with Bolognese Sauce, Parmesan cheese, Roasted Garlic, Romaine salad with Lemon Parmesan Dressing, Crusty Peasant Bread with Caramelized Onions, Butterscotch-Topped Gingerbread with Sautéed Apples

Thursday:

It's early morning yet, but excitement starts to build as Cap'n Jon returns from an early trip with a crate full of fresh lobsters. After breakfast *Pearl* ferries us ashore to Stonington. Stonington, on the southern tip of Deer Isle, is aptly named. There is abundant evidence in town and on the surrounding islands of the granite quarries that were a mainstay for the town in the 19th century. Nowadays the residents of Stonington earn a living from lobstering and a few craft shops.

The oldest kids we know, and a magical couple, Jan and Evelyn Kok have been welcoming and entertaining windjammer passengers for decades in their tiny, eclectic shop in Stonington. Both are artists – Jan a music director and Evelyn an illustrator. Their shop is full of fascinating artwork and knick-knacks. Very little of it is for sale, but Evelyn makes beautiful bookmarks featuring all the schooners as well as a number of beautiful line drawings. It's wonderful to poke around while Evelyn hand-letters passengers' names on the bookmarks, and it's not at all unusual for Jan and Evelyn to break into one of their songs – it feels like you've walked into a pixie's tea party!

After a leisurely morning ashore we weigh anchor, raise sails, and we're off, cruising among the islands of Merchant's Row. We see a pod of dolphins appear among the waves – cameras and binoculars are quickly pulled out. We anchor early near the sandy beach of Lindy Cove for our lobster bake. There's no rush as we have plenty of time to explore the island before we settle down to all the lobster we can eat. The last boatload of passengers returns to the *Riggin* at dusk. We got a little extra sun today and everyone is happy and full. We watch as the stars come out, and have an impromptu star-gazing session, picking out the Big and Little Dipper, Cassiopeia and the Summer Triangle.

This book is being read by Jon and Annie Happy Anniversary schooner J. & E. Riggin off Stonington, Maine

Lobsterbake

The highlight of the week for many of our passengers is our traditional Maine lobster bake – a feature of all our weeklong trips. It's an all-you-can-eat feast; seven lobsters eaten by one person in one sitting is the record (please do not try this at home). After anchoring near an undisturbed island in the early afternoon, the yawl boat ferries us ashore and we hop across granite rocks to the beach. Everyone wanders off in different directions – exploring inland, walking the shore, swimming – some even help set up for dinner.

The crew has already rowed ashore and brought everything we need to the island:

* Firewood (we bring it with us instead of collecting driftwood so we make the least impact on the island's ecosystem)
* Fire pan (we build the fire on top of this pan)
* Galvanized steel washtub
* Lobsters
* Mussels and clams
* Fresh corn on the cob
* Baked potatoes
* Melted lemon butter
* Snacks
* Watermelon
* Lemonade (passengers often bring beer or wine with them)
* Sausages and chicken (for non-lobster fans)
* Chocolate bars, marshmallows and graham crackers

A Tasty Accident

One time a passenger made a delightful mistake. She and her husband were celebrating their wedding anniversary and were drinking a celebratory glass of champagne. It was nestled right next to the butter cup and she accidentally dipped her lobster into the champagne. It was delicious – and low fat!

A fire is lit below the high tide mark, corn is shucked, various goodies are put out to tide us over until the lobster is ready. Once the fire is really going the lobster pot – a huge steel tub – is filled with 2-3 inches of salt water and set on the fire to boil. While we wait for the water to come to a boil, several armloads of sea-weed are gathered (we're careful to leave some seaweed at each spot so it can grow back). Once the water is boiling we layer the lobsters, corn, mussels, and clams in the pot, cover it with a "lid" of seaweed, wait for it to come to a boil, and rotate the pot (for even cooking on the fire). When the water comes to second boil we'll pull some of the seaweed aside and check to see that the lobsters are red all over. When the lobsters are done, the pot is carried away from the fire, the seaweed is arranged on flat rock, and everything is placed on the seaweed bed, ready to eat!

Once everyone has had their fill of lobster, the water-melon is sliced and the makings for S'mores are laid out. There's always a lively discussion over how to make

the best S'more, and the proper way to roast a marshmallow. Below is our recipe for S'mores:

Hershey® bar
1 full graham cracker, broken in half
2 marshmallows

Place the Hershey bar on top of one of the halves of graham cracker and place it on a rock near the fire so the chocolate can get warm.

Place two marshmallows on a metal roasting stick (not driftwood) and slowly turn it over the hot coals until it becomes brown. It's important to take your time here as the impatient folks end up with a burnt marshmallow. Some poor souls actually like them this way – go figure.

Slide the marshmallows on top of the chocolate and complete the sandwich by placing the second graham cracker on top of the marshmallows.

Leave No Trace

While we are on an island for our lobster bake we operate under a Leave No Trace policy. Whatever we take onto the island, we take off. Often we leave with more than we came with, as picking up litter while exploring an island is our contribution to leaving an island better than we found it. Our fires are built below the high tide line; five minutes after we've left an island, you can't tell we've been there.

Thursday Menu

Breakfast – Granola, yogurt, cottage cheese, hard-boiled eggs, Apricot Coffee Cake, dried fruit, fresh fruit

Lunch – Chicken, Roasted Red Pepper and Couscous Salad, Roasted Beet Salad, Israeli Couscous and Fruit Salad, Newfi Bread, Mom's Chocolate Cake

Dinner – Lobster Bake with steamed lobster, clams and corn; baked potatoes, crudités, fire-grilled chicken, trail mix, watermelon, S'mores, and lemonade

Friday

As the week goes by everyone relaxes more and more and rises later and later. But coffee is still ready at 7 for early risers, and several passengers take our peapod out for a quiet row.

By Friday everyone is an ol' salt and is ready help get the Riggin underway; the Captain calls out "Heave out!" and "Raise your headsails!" and we're off for our final full day of sailing. We head westward, back towards Rockland. Sailing off the anchor powered by wind alone. No sound of an engine, no smell of diesel fumes, just the water lapping on the hull. With a brisk wind, we sail through the Fox Islands Thoroughfare, a picturesque passageway between Vinal Haven Island and North Haven Island, and then tack out the east side. We turn North and, as the afternoon sea breeze fills our sails, shoot up the coast of North Haven to our final stop for the trip, Pulpit Harbor. Records of the osprey nest that stands sentry at the entrance of Pulpit Harbor go back over 200 years. It's a real treat to sit at anchor and watch these majestic birds fish for their dinners. It's been an exciting week!

Friday Menu

Breakfast – French Toast with Raspberry Jam and Cream Cheese Filling, Blueberry Syrup, bacon, and melon wedges

Lunch – Black bean chili, Pico de Gallo, Golden Corn Bread, grated cheddar cheese, diced onions, sour cream, tortilla chips, carrots, celery sticks and brownies

Appetizer –Lobster Dip, local cheeses, homemade Crostini and black and green olives

Dinner – Roasted Pork Loin with Cranberry Port Sauce, Potatoes Roasted with Red Wine, steamed green beans, roasted onions, Focaccia, Chocolate Decadence Pie

Saturday :

Saturday morning we raise anchor early and head back home. Last minute group photos are taken, addresses exchanged, and a hearty brunch is served to tide everyone over on their way home. We tie up in Rockland amid relaxed, revitalized smiles and see everyone ashore with hugs and goodbyes.

Saturday Menu

Brunch: Sticky Buns, Frittata, corned beef hash, fruit salad, Granola, juice.

Cranberry Bread

2 cups all-purpose flour
$^1/_2$ teaspoon salt
$1^1/_2$ teaspoons baking powder
$^1/_2$ teaspoon baking soda
1 cup sugar
1 large egg, beaten
3 tablespoons shortening, melted
$^3/_4$ cup orange juice
$^1/_2$ cup nuts (optional)
2 cups cranberries
Grated rind of 1 orange

* Preheat oven to 350°. Grease a loaf pan.
* Sift the dry ingredients together in a large bowl.
* Stir the egg, melted shortening, and orange juice into the dry ingredients until barely mixed in.
* Fold in the nuts, cranberries, and orange rind.
* Bake for 50 minutes or until the bread springs back when lightly pressed.
* Cool in pan.

Crossroads Banana Bread

4 ripe bananas, peeled and mashed
1 teaspoon lemon juice
1 cup sugar
$^1/_2$ cup shortening
2 large eggs
2 tablespoons buttermilk
2 cups all-purpose flour
$^1/_2$ teaspoon salt
1 teaspoon baking soda
2 teaspoons baking powder

※ Preheat oven to 350°. Grease one loaf pan.

※ In a small bowl, pour the lemon juice and buttermilk over the mashed bananas; set aside.

※ In a large bowl beat the sugar, shortening and eggs until fluffy. Stir in the milk.

※ In a separate bowl, mix together the flour, baking soda and salt.

※ Mix about $^1/_3$ of the flour mixture into the sugar and egg mixture, then mix in about $^1/_3$ of the banana/milk mixture. Repeat two more times until everything is mixed in.

※ Bake for 1 hour, or until a fork comes out clean. Cool for 20 minutes in the pan before removing.

Golden Northern Cornbread

1 cup yellow or white stone-ground corn meal
1 cup all-purpose flour
2 teaspoons baking powder
$^1/_2$ teaspoon baking soda
4 teaspoons sugar
$^1/_2$ teaspoon salt
2 large eggs
$^2/_3$ cup buttermilk
$^2/_3$ cup milk
2 tablespoons unsalted butter, melted

* Adjust oven rack to center position and preheat the oven to 425°. Grease a cast iron skillet or 9 x 9-inch baking pan.
* Stir the cornmeal, flour, baking powder, baking soda, sugar, and salt in large bowl. Make a well in the center of the dry ingredients.
* Add the eggs into the well and stir lightly with wooden spoon; then add the buttermilk and milk. Stir quickly until almost combined.
* Add the melted butter and stir until the ingredients are just combined.
* Pour the batter into the greased pan. Bake until the top is golden brown and lightly cracked and the edges have pulled away from side of the pan, about 25 minutes.
* Transfer the pan to a wire rack to cool for around 5-10 minutes. Cut into squares and serve warm.

Herb-Cheese Bread

3 cups all-purpose flour
$^1/_2$ cup packed brown sugar
2 tablespoons shortening
1 teaspoon baking soda
1 teaspoon baking powder
1 teaspoon salt
$^2/_3$ cup sour milk
$^2/_3$ cup grated cheddar cheese
$^2/_3$ cup cottage cheese
2 large eggs
1 teaspoon dried dill
$^1/_2$ teaspoon dried basil
$^1/_2$ teaspoon dried tarragon
$^1/_2$ teaspoon dried oregano

✳ Preheat oven to 350°. Grease one loaf pan.
✳ In a large bowl, sift together the dry ingredients.
✳ Make a well, then add the remaining ingredients and stir until just mixed.
✳ Spoon the mixture into the prepared pan and bake for 45 to 55 minutes.

Irish Soda Bread

4 cups sifted all-purpose flour
2 teaspoons salt
1$^1/_2$ teaspoons baking soda
1$^1/_2$ teaspoons cream of tartar
$^1/_2$ cup sugar
2 tablespoons caraway seeds
1 cup currants
1 cups sour milk

* Preheat oven to 350°.
* In a large bowl, sift together the flour, salt, baking soda, and cream of tartar.
* Mix in the sugar, caraway seeds and raisins.
* Stir in the milk until a ball forms.
* Turn onto floured board and knead until smooth (about 5-10 turns).
* Cut the dough in half and shape into two 6" round loaves.
* Place the loaves on the cookie pan. Make two cuts on top of the loaves in the shape of a cross.
* Bake for 40 minutes.

Mom & Grandma's Brown Bread   *Makes 1 loaf*

This was my grandmother's recipe. The original recipe called for graham flour and sour milk. I've substituted whole wheat flour and buttermilk.

2 tablespoons shortening
$^1/_2$ cup packed light brown sugar
1 cup all-purpose flour
2 cups whole wheat.
1 teaspoon baking soda
1 teaspoon baking powder
1 teaspoon salt
2 cups buttermilk
2 large eggs, beaten
3 tablespoons molasses

* Preheat oven to 375°. Grease one loaf pan.
* Cream together the shortening and sugar.
* Add the milk, eggs, and molasses and stir until just mixed.
* Stir in the flours, baking soda, baking powder, and salt.
* Pour into the greased pan, and let it sit 20-30 minutes.
* Bake for 45 minutes to an hour, until a knife inserted in the center of the loaf comes out clean.
* Cool in the pan.

Lorraine's Nectarine-Blueberry Bread

Makes 1 loaf

Lorraine, one of the owners of the *Victory Chimes*, gave this recipe to me when I was running the galley for them.

Bread:

3/4 cup sugar
1/3 cup butter
2 large eggs
1 1/2 cups all-purpose flour
1/2 teaspoon ground allspice
1/4 teaspoon baking soda
1 teaspoon grated orange rind
1 medium nectarine, peeled and cut into -inch pieces
1 cup fresh blueberries

Almond and Sugar Topping:

2/3 cup chopped almonds
1 tablespoon sugar

* Preheat oven to 350°. Grease one loaf pan.
* Cream the sugar and butter together in a bowl.
* Add the eggs and mix well.
* Sift all the dry ingredients on top of the mixture and mix until just blended.
* Gently stir in the fruit.
* Pour the batter into the loaf pan.
* Mix the almonds and sugar together and sprinkle the mixture over the batter.
* Bake until the bread springs back when gently pressed (about 1 hour).

Poppy Seed Bread

This recipe is based on one given to me by CIA alumna and former schooner chef Dana Degenhardt. I often use this recipe as a lunch dessert. I pour the batter into a 9 x 13-inch pan and make a cake. You can make muffins with this recipe as well.

Bread:

3 cups all-purpose flour
$1^1/_2$ teaspoons salt
$1^1/_2$ teaspoons baking powder
$2^1/_2$ cups sugar
$1^1/_2$ cups milk
3 large eggs, beaten
1 cup vegetable oil
5 tablespoons whole dry poppy seeds
2 teaspoons vanilla extract
2 teaspoons almond extract

Glaze:

$^3/_4$ cup sugar
$^1/_4$ cup orange juice
$^1/_2$ teaspoon vanilla extract
$^1/_2$ teaspoon almond extract
2 teaspoons butter

Bread:

※ Preheat oven to 350°. Grease two loaf pans.
※ In a large bowl, sift together the flour, salt, baking powder, and sugar.
※ Add the remaining bread ingredients and beat for 2 minutes.
※ Divide the batter into the greased loaf pans; bake until bread springs back when lightly pressed, about 1 hour 15 minutes.

Glaze:

※ Bring all the glaze ingredients to a boil; reduce heat and simmer until the sugar dissolves.
※ Pour the glaze over the hot bread while the bread is still in the pan.
※ Cool completely before removing it from the pan.

Pumpkin Bread

When I make this for a special afternoon tea, I replace $^1/_3$ cup orange juice with $^1/_3$ cup Grand Marnier.

$^2/_3$ cup shortening
$2^2/_3$ cups sugar
4 eggs
1 16-ounce can pumpkin
$^2/_3$ cup orange juice (or $^1/_3$ cup orange juice and $^1/_3$ cup Grand Marnier)
$3^1/_3$ cups all-purpose flour
2 teaspoons baking soda
$1^1/_2$ teaspoons salt
$^1/_2$ teaspoon baking powder
1 teaspoon cinnamon
1 teaspoon cloves
1 cup currants or raisins (optional)

✳ Preheat the oven to 350°. Grease 1 loaf pan.

✳ Cream the shortening and sugar together.

✳ Add the eggs, pumpkin, juice and optional liquor and mix thoroughly.

✳ Sift the dry ingredients into the bowl and stir until just mixed.

✳ Pour the batter into the loaf pan; bake until the bread springs back when lightly pressed (about 1 hour).

Spiced Apple Muffins

$^1/_4$ cup raisins
$^1/_4$ cup currants
$^1/_4$ cup rum or sherry
$1^1/_2$ cups all-purpose flour
$^1/_2$ teaspoon salt
$^1/_2$ teaspoon baking soda
$^1/_2$ teaspoon ground cinnamon
Pinch ground cardamom
$^3/_4$ cup vegetable oil
1 cup sugar
1 large egg
$^1/_2$ teaspoon vanilla extract
2 small apples, peeled, cored, and roughly chopped
$^1/_2$ cup coarsely chopped walnuts

* Soak the raisins and currants in the rum at least 1 hour, or as long as overnight.
* Preheat oven to 350°. Grease muffin pans.
* In a large bowl, mix together the dry ingredients.
* Add the oil, sugar, eggs, and vanilla extract. Mix until just incorporated into the dry ingredients.
* Stir in the apples and walnuts.
* Fill muffin cups ²/₃ full with the batter.
* Bake about 25 minutes, until the muffins spring back when lightly pressed.
* Remove the muffins from the pans to cool.

Zucchini Bread

3 large eggs, beaten
1 cup vegetable oil
2 cups sugar
2 cups grated zucchini
2 teaspoons vanilla extract
3 cups all-purpose flour
1 teaspoon baking soda
$^1/_2$ teaspoon baking powder
1 teaspoon salt
1 teaspoon ground cinnamon
$^1/_2$ cup coarsely chopped nuts (walnuts, pecans, etc.)

* Preheat oven to 325°. Grease two loaf pans.
* In a large bowl thoroughly mix the oil, sugar, zucchini, and vanilla extract. Add all the remaining ingredients except the nuts. Mix well.
* Stir in the nuts.
* Divide into the greased loaf pans.
* Bake about one hour, until the bread springs back when lightly pressed.
* Cool in the pan.

Sweet Endings

Bars and Cookies

The recipes in this chapter are very versatile. For example, the Raspberry Bars can be used for a picnic lunch, but drizzle some chocolate on top and add some hazelnuts and they become a wonderful afternoon treat with coffee or tea. The Congo Bars are by far the favorite on board and the Brownies are a close second. The Ginger Shortbread is also popular and one that is so easy it's usually my Monday dessert. We'll serve these for dessert at lunch and then leave them out all afternoon for folks to munch on. They are almost always gone by dinner!

I've adapted this recipe from my friend Ellen's brownie recipe. It has a deep, rich flavor (the coffee granules are the secret ingredient!).

8 ounces unsweetened chocolate
1 cup (2 sticks) butter
5 large eggs
1 tablespoon pure vanilla extract
1 teaspoon pure almond extract
$^1/_4$ teaspoon salt
$2^1/_2$ tablespoons instant coffee granules
$3^3/_4$ cups sugar
$1^2/_3$ cups all-purpose flour
1 cup walnuts (optional)

✳ Preheat oven to 400°. Line a 9 x 9-inch baking pan with aluminum foil then grease the foil with butter.
✳ Melt the chocolate and butter in double boiler until the chocolate is almost melted. Remove from heat and stir occasionally until the chocolate is completely melted and the mixture has cooled to room temperature.
✳ In a large mixing bowl, beat together the eggs, vanilla extract, almond extract, salt, coffee and sugar.
✳ Add the chocolate/butter mixture and stir.
✳ Stir in the flour and mix until blended.
✳ Stir in the walnuts.
✳ Spread the batter evenly in the prepared pan.
✳ Bake 35 minutes.
✳ Cool; while still warm, cut into squares.

This is one that my family would make every Christmas. My brothers and I could eat a pan of these in no time flat.

Bars:

2/3 cup shortening
4 squares chocolate
2 cups packed light brown sugar
3 large eggs
1 teaspoon vanilla extract
1$^1/_4$ cups all-purpose flour
1 teaspoon baking powder
$^1/_2$ teaspoon salt

Frosting:

2 cups confectioner's sugar
$^1/_4$ cup ($^1/_2$ stick) softened butter
2 tablespoons milk or cream
$^3/_4$ teaspoon peppermint extract

Glaze:

2 squares unsweetened chocolate
2 tablespoons butter

* Preheat oven to 350°. Grease a 9 x 13-inch baking pan.
* Melt the shortening and chocolate in a double boiler. Cool.
* Beat in the sugar, eggs and vanilla.
* Sift in the dry ingredients and mix well.
* Bake for 25-30 minutes, until a fork inserted in the bars comes out clean. Cool in the pan.
* Beat the frosting ingredients together until light and creamy then frost the bars.
* Melt the glaze ingredients in a double boiler, cool slightly then pour the glaze over the frosting. Tilt the pan to spread the glaze.
* Cut into bars.

Congo Squares

This is a recipe from the *Stephen Taber*. Ellen says the first time she made it, it was so gooey that she wanted to throw them out. A passenger saw her and grabbed the pan out of her hands. Half an hour later Ellen had a bunch of happy passengers and an empty pan. That's the way we've baked them ever since; this recipe is much better slightly underdone than even the smallest bit overdone.

$2^1/_3$ cups brown sugar
$^3/_4$ cup ($1^1/_2$ sticks) butter
$^1/_2$ teaspoon vanilla extract
3 large eggs
$2^1/_4$ cups all-purpose flour
$2^1/_2$ teaspoons baking powder
$^1/_2$ teaspoon salt
1 cup chocolate chips
1 cup chopped walnuts

* Preheat oven to 350°. Grease a 9 x 13-inch pan.
* Melt the brown sugar and butter over low heat.
* Cool slightly, add the vanilla extract, then beat in the eggs one at a time.
* Stir in the flour, baking powder and salt; when the dry ingredients are completely incorporated, add the chocolate chips and walnuts.
* Spread the dough evenly onto the greased pan and bake for 30 minutes. If a fork poked into the center comes out slightly gooey this is okay.
* Cool slightly and cut into squares while still warm.

Cranberry-Almond Biscotti

Makes 2 dozen

A passenger of ours, Lauren Hubbell, gave this recipe to me. To dress them up a bit, dip one end of the biscotti into melted semi-sweet chocolate and place on waxed paper to cool. Biscotti are crunchy and store well. They're excellent for dipping into coffee, hot cocoa, or whatever you'd like.

$2^1/_4$ cups all-purpose flour
1 cup sugar
1 teaspoon baking powder
$^1/_2$ teaspoon baking soda
4 large eggs
1 teaspoon vanilla extract
$1^1/_4$ cups dried cranberries
1 cup whole almonds

✳ Preheat oven to 325°. Grease one cookie pan.
✳ Mix together all the ingredients. The dough will be stiff and sticky.
✳ Grease your hands well and form the dough into 2 logs (1 x 2 x 15 inches) place on the greased cookie pan.
✳ Bake for 30 minutes.
✳ Remove the logs from pan to rack and cool for 5-10 minutes.
✳ Reduce the oven temperature to 300°.
✳ While still warm, slice the logs at an angle into -inch slices. Place the slices on an ungreased cookie pan and bake for an additional 20 minutes.
✳ Remove from pan and cool on rack.

1 cup (2 sticks) unsalted butter, softened
1 cup confectioner's sugar
2 teaspoons vanilla extract
2 cups all-purpose flour
$1/_4$ teaspoon salt
$1/_4$ cup chopped crystallized ginger

✳ Preheat oven to 350°

✳ Cream the butter in a medium bowl.

✳ Beat in the sugar and vanilla.

✳ Mix in the flour and salt; it's easiest to finish mixing the dough with your hands.

✳ Stir in the ginger.

✳ Pat the dough into a 9-inch round cake pan.

✳ Score it into wedges with a sharp knife.

✳ Bake about 20 to 30 minutes, until the shortbread is a pale golden brown.

✳ Cool in the pan; while still warm, cut along the score lines.

Variations
After the dough has been made, you can replace the ginger with any number of ingredients. These are some of my favorites.
Chocolate chip – 1 cup chocolate chips.
Walnut – Mix 1 cup finely chopped walnuts into the dough. After the dough is in the pan, press $1/_4$ cup coarsely broken walnuts into the dough.
You can do the same thing with almonds, or any nuts.
Ginger-Orange – Add 1 tablespoon orange zest and $1/_4$ cup chopped crystallized ginger.
Lemon – Add 1 tablespoon lemon zest.

Grandma's Ginger Cookies

You can also use this recipe to make bars – simply spread the dough evenly in a greased 9 x 13-inch pan and bake at 350° for around 30-40 minutes. We usually make bar cookies on the boat, but I'll make these for the crew if they roll them and dust them with sugar.

$^3/_4$ cup shortening
1 cup packed light brown sugar
1 large egg
$^1/_4$ cup molasses
$^1/_4$ teaspoon salt
$2^1/_4$ cups all-purpose flour
2 teaspoons baking soda
$^1/_2$ teaspoon ground cloves
1 teaspoon ground cinnamon
1 teaspoon powdered ginger
Granulated sugar as needed

✳ Preheat the oven to 375°.
✳ In a large bowl, mix together the shortening, brown sugar, egg, and molasses. Mix in the remaining ingredients.
✳ Roll the dough into 1-inch balls, roll them in the sugar, then place them on an ungreased cookie pan.
✳ Bake for 10 minutes; cool on a rack.

Thick & Chewy Double Chocolate Cookies *Makes 2 dozen*

You can also use this recipe to make bars – simply spread the dough evenly in a greased 9 x 13-inch pan and bake at 350° for about 30 to 40 minutes.

16 ounces semisweet chocolate (either chips or coarsely chopped)
4 large eggs
2 teaspoons vanilla extract
2 teaspoons instant coffee or espresso powder
10 tablespoons unsalted butter, softened
$1^1/_2$ cups packed brown sugar
$^1/_2$ cup sugar
2 cups all-purpose flour
$^1/_2$ cup Dutch cocoa powder
2 teaspoons baking powder
1 teaspoon salt

✳ Preheat oven to 350°.
✳ Melt the chocolate in a microwave or double boiler. Set aside to cool slightly.
✳ In a small bowl, beat the eggs and vanilla lightly with fork; sprinkle in the coffee powder and stir until dissolved. Set aside.
✳ In a large bowl, beat the butter until smooth and creamy. Add both sugars and beat until creamy.
✳ Gradually beat in the egg mixture.
✳ Add the chocolate and beat until combined.
✳ Sift the flour, cocoa, baking powder, and salt into the mixture and beat until just combined. Do not overmix.
✳ Cover with plastic wrap and let stand at room temperature until it firms up to a fudge-like consistency.
✳ Line 2 cookie pans with parchment paper. Form 1-inch balls and place them $1^1/_2$ inches apart on the cookie pan.
✳ Bake about 10 minutes, turning the cookie pans about halfway through. Cool on racks.

Charlie Who?

Charlie Noble is an "it," not a "he;" it's the nickname for the galley smokestack. A British merchant service captain, Charles Noble, is said to be responsible for the origin of the name around 1850. It seems that upon discovering that the stack of his ship's galley was made of copper, Captain Noble ordered that it be kept brightly polished. The ship's crew then started referring to the stack as the "Charley Noble."

Hello Dolly Bars

Makes 24 bars

We also called these Everything-But-the-Kitchen-Sink Bars.

$^1/_2$ cup (1 stick) butter, melted
1 cup crushed vanilla wafers or graham crackers
6 ounces (small bag) chocolate chips
6 ounces (small bag) butterscotch chips
1 cup shredded coconut
1 cup chopped nuts (pecan, almonds, walnuts)
1 can sweetened condensed milk

✳ Preheat oven to 350°.
✳ Pour the melted butter into a 9 x 13-inch pan.
✳ Sprinkle the crushed vanilla wafers evenly over the butter.
✳ Sprinkle the chocolate chips in an even layer over the wafers.
✳ Repeat with the butterscotch chips, coconut and nuts.
✳ Pour the condensed milk evenly over the nuts.
✳ Bake for 20 minutes, cool slightly, and cut while still warm.

Lemon Bars

Base:

3 cups all-purpose flour
1^1/$_3$ cups confectioner's sugar
^{1}/$_2$ cup cornstarch
1^1/$_2$ teaspoons salt
1^1/$_2$ cups (3 sticks) unsalted butter, room temperature, cut into chunks

Filling:

8 large eggs, lightly beaten
2^2/$_3$ cups granulated sugar
6 tablespoons all-purpose flour
1^1/$_3$ cups fresh lemon juice (three lemons)
^{2}/$_3$ cup whole milk
^{1}/$_8$ teaspoon salt
Confectioner's sugar for dusting

✳ Preheat oven to 350°. Butter a 9 x 13-inch pan.

✳ By hand or with a pastry blender or food processor, combine the base ingredients until they are the consistency of coarse meal.

✳ Press the mixture firmly into the buttered pan.

✳ Bake 20 minutes.

✳ Whisk together the eggs, sugar, and flour; then stir in the lemon juice, milk, and salt.

✳ Reduce oven temperature to 325°. Pour the filling over the warm crust and bake an additional 20 minutes.

✳ Cool completely and cut into bars. Dust with the confectioner's sugar.

Mandel Balchen

This recipe was given to me by former schooner chef Dana Degenhardt. The cookies are delicate and rich, perfect for an afternoon tea.

$3^1/_2$ ounces bittersweet chocolate pieces
6 tablespoons soft butter
$^3/_4$ cup confectioner's sugar
$^1/_4$ teaspoon almond extract
$^3/_4$ cup very finely ground almonds

* Melt the chocolate in a double boiler; set aside to cool slightly.
* In a medium bowl beat the butter and sugar until very creamy and smooth.
* Stir in the melted chocolate and almond extract.
* Stir in the almonds.
* Form the dough into a ball, wrap it in plastic wrap, and chill it for 1 hour.
* Preheat oven to 175° (yes, really – 175°).
* Pinch off about 1 teaspoon of the dough; roll into a ball, and place it on an ungreased cookie pan (you'll probably need two pans).
* Bake for 50 minutes. Turn off the oven but leave the pans in the closed oven for 1 hour.
* Gently remove the cookies from the pan. Store in an airtight container.

Raspberry Bars

1$^1/_2$ cups (3 sticks) unsalted butter, room temperature
1$^1/_4$ cups sugar
1 large egg
2$^1/_4$ cups all-purpose flour
1 cup raspberry preserves

* Preheat oven to 350°. Butter a 9 x 13-inch baking pan.
* Cream together the butter and sugar.
* Stir in the egg until completely incorporated
* Stir in the flour.
* Press half of the dough into the prepared pan.
* Spread the jam evenly on top of the dough; crumble the remaining dough over the preserves as evenly as possible.
* Bake about 30 minutes, until the top is golden brown.
* Cool in the pan and cut.

Kool-Aid® "Play Dough®"

This recipe smells good, but doesn't taste good, so the kids won't eat it. The salt is a preservative so it will keep for a long time.

2½ cups flour
1 cup salt
2 packets unsweetened Kool-Aid®
2 cups water
1 tablespoon vegetable oil

Blend all the dry ingredients together in a bowl.
Bring the water to a boil, add the oil to the water, and then mix it thoroughly into the dry mixture.
Store it in a plastic bag or airtight container.

Triple Ginger Biscotti

Makes around 2 dozen

This recipe was given to me by passenger Robin Romero.

$^3/_4$ cup whole almonds
$^1/_2$ cup (1stick) butter
$^3/_4$ cup packed dark brown sugar
2 tablespoons molasses
2 large eggs
$2^1/_4$ cups all-purpose flour
2 teaspoons ground ginger
$1^1/_2$ teaspoons baking powder
$^1/_4$ teaspoon salt
2 tablespoons peeled and chopped fresh ginger root
$^2/3$ cup finely chopped crystallized ginger

✳ Bake the almonds in a 350° oven until brown, around 8-10 minutes. Cool, then cut them in halves or thirds.
✳ Reduce heat to 325°.
✳ Cream the butter and sugar until light and fluffy.
✳ Beat in the molasses and eggs.
✳ Combine the dry ingredients in a separate bowl then stir them into the butter/sugar mixture.
✳ Stir in the fresh and crystallized gingers.
✳ Fold in the almonds.
✳ Divide the dough in half.
✳ Form the dough into 2 logs about half an inch thick, $1^1/_2$ inches wide and 14 inches long.
✳ Place the logs, about 2 inches apart, on an ungreased cookie pan and bake until golden brown (about 25 minutes).
✳ Cool for 5 minutes; with a serrated knife, cut the logs diagonally into $^1/_2$-inch slices.
✳ Lay the slices on a cookie pan and return to the oven for 10 minutes, turning them over once. Cool on rack.

Pies and Cakes

Some of my favorite shipboard memories are of times when we are at anchor, the awning is up, the decks are cleared and dinner is over. Jon and I are able to sit and look out over the harbor and watch the sunset with our passengers as we enjoy our after dinner coffee and dessert.

Almost all of these desserts are either classics or classics with a twist. They are tried and true. I can always depend on them working time after time. If you just want a traditional recipe without the extras, it's easy enough to skip the parts that are "twists." For example if you just want to make Banana Cream Pie, just leave out the parts with the chocolate. If you'd like a simple gingerbread, leave off the Apple Topping in Butterscotch-Topped Gingerbread.

Apricot-Ginger Pound Cake with Rum Glaze

Makes 12-16 servings

$1^1/_2$ cups (3 sticks) unsalted butter, very soft
3 cups sugar
7 large eggs
$1^1/_2$ teaspoons vanilla extract
$^1/_3$ cup sour cream
$^1/_3$ cup milk
$3^1/_2$ cups all-purpose flour
$^3/_4$ teaspoon salt
$^1/_2$ teaspoon baking powder
$^1/_4$ cup coarsely chopped crystallized ginger
$^1/_2$ cup coarsely chopped dried apricots

Glaze:

2 tablespoons dark rum
2 tablespoons orange juice
$^3/_4$ cup sugar

✳ Have all ingredients at room temperature.

✳ Preheat oven to 325°. Butter and flour a bundt pan.

✳ Place the butter and sugar in the bowl of an electric mixer. Cream them together at medium speed, then add the eggs, vanilla, sour cream and milk.

✳ Add the flour, salt and baking powder and beat on low speed until creamy and smooth, around $1^1/_2$ to 2 minutes, stopping occasionally to scrape the bowl.

✳ Gently fold in the ginger and apricots by hand.

✳ Spread the batter evenly in the prepared pan and bake until the cake springs back when lightly touched in the center, approximately 1 hour 10 minutes.

✳ Cool the cake upright on a cooling rack for about 10 minutes.

✳ Tap the sides and invert the cake onto the cooling rack.

✳ In a small bowl, blend together the rum, orange juice and sugar. Use a pastry brush to brush the surface of the warm cake with the glaze. Allow the glazed cake to cool completely before serving (approximately 1 to 2 hours).

Beiler's 5-Flavor Pound Cake

While all of these extracts are not what most folks normally have on hand, they make all the difference. I was able to find them all at my local grocery store. This recipe was given to me by an exceptional family that sailed with us one year. They own a bakery in Amish country.

$^3/_4$ cup ($1^1/_2$ sticks) butter, softened
$1^1/_2$ cups sugar
2 large eggs (if double then 5 eggs)
$1^1/_2$ cups all-purpose flour
$^1/_4$ teaspoon baking powder
$^1/_4$ teaspoon salt
$^1/_2$ cup milk
$^1/_2$ teaspoon vanilla extract
$^1/_2$ teaspoon lemon extract
$^1/_2$ teaspoon butter extract
$^1/_2$ teaspoon rum extract
$^1/_4$ teaspoon coconut extract

Glaze:

$^1/_2$ cup sugar
$^1/_4$ cup water
$^1/_2$ teaspoon vanilla extract
$^1/_2$ teaspoon lemon extract
$^1/_2$ teaspoon butter extract
$^1/_2$ teaspoon rum extract
$^1/_4$ teaspoon coconut extract

* Preheat oven to 350°. Grease one loaf pan.
* In a large bowl, cream together the butter and sugar, then add the eggs.
* Sift in the flour, baking powder and salt into a separate bowl.
* Mix the milk and extracts together in a third bowl.
* Add half of the flour mixture and half of the milk mixture to the first bowl and mix until incorporated.
* Repeat and pour into the prepared pan. Bake for about 1 hour and 15 minutes, until a fork inserted in the center of the cake comes clean.

Glaze:

* Bring all the glaze ingredients to a boil; pour it over the cake just as it comes out of the oven. Let the cake cool a bit before removing it from the pan.

Berry Pie

1 9-inch baked pie shell (page 200)
4 cups fresh blueberries or mixed berries
1 cup sugar
2 tablespoons cornstarch; 3 if the berries are juicy

✳ Preheat oven to 350°.

✳ Roll out the piecrust and place it in a 9-inch pie pan. Freeze it for 15 minutes then cover the bottom of the crust with dried beans (to keep it flat while it bakes) and bake until set – about 10 to 15 minutes. Cool completely.

✳ Place 2 cups of berries in the baked pie shell.

✳ Mash 2 cups of berries and combine them in a saucepan with the sugar and cornstarch; boil the mixture over medium-high heat until the liquid is thick and clear.

✳ Pour the hot mixture over the berries in the pie shell and spread evenly.

✳ Cool and serve with whipped cream or ice cream.

Black Bottom Banana Cream Pie

1 pie crust (use the recipe on page 200 or a store-bought crust)

Ganache:

4 ounces bittersweet chocolate, coarsely chopped
6 tablespoons whipping cream
2 tablespoons unsalted butter
2 large, firm, ripe bananas, peeled and cut into $^2/_3$-inch slices

Filling:

$1^1/_2$ teaspoons pure vanilla extract
$1^1/_2$ teaspoons dark rum
1 teaspoon unflavored gelatin
$^1/_2$ cup whipping cream
5 large egg yolks
3 tablespoons sugar
$^1/_2$ cup chilled whipping cream

Topping

$^3/_4$ cup chilled whipping cream
2 tablespoons sugar
2 firm ripe bananas

* Preheat oven to 350°.
* Roll out the piecrust and place it in a 9-inch pie pan. Freeze it for 15 minutes then cover the bottom of the crust with dried beans (to keep it flat while it bakes) and bake until set – about 10 to 15 minutes. Cool completely.

Ganache:

* Make a ganache by heating the chocolate, cream, and butter over a double boiler until melted and smooth.
* Spread 6 tablespoons of the ganache onto the bottom of the cooled crust.
* Cool slightly and press the bananas into the ganache.

Filling:

* Combine vanilla and rum together and sprinkle gelatin over the mixture. Let stand 10 minutes.
* Bring the whipping cream to a simmer. Whisk the egg yolks and sugar together in a separate bowl; then slowly whisk the mixture into the cream.

✳ Stir the mixture over low heat until it thickens to a ribbon-like consistency, then add the gelatin mixture.

✳ Chill, stirring occasionally until cool, but not set (approximately 20 minutes). Whip the $^1/_2$ cup whipped cream: fold half of the whipped cream into the custard, then repeat with the remaining whipped cream. Spoon the mixture into the pie crust; refrigerate for 2 hours.

✳ Stir the reserved ganache over low heat. Spread on top of the custard and chill.

Topping:

✳ Whip together the cream and sugar and top the pie with whipped cream and bananas.

Butterscotch-Topped Gingerbread with Sautéed Apples

Makes 12 servings

6 tablespoons unsalted butter
$^3/_4$ cup packed brown sugar
$2^3/_4$ cups cake flour
1 teaspoon baking powder
$^1/_2$ teaspoon baking soda
$^1/_4$ teaspoon salt
1 tablespoon ground ginger
1 tablespoon ground cinnamon
$^1/_4$ teaspoon ground cloves
$^1/_2$ cup (1 stick) unsalted butter, softened
$^1/_2$ cup sugar
1 teaspoon baking soda
1 cup molasses
$1^1/_2$ cups boiling water
2 large eggs

Apple Topping:

3 tablespoons unsalted butter
2 tablespoons sugar
4 medium apples, peeled, cored, and cut into $^1/_4$-inch wedges
Whipped cream for garnish

* Preheat oven to 300°.
* Butter and flour the sides (not the bottom) of a nine-inch round cake pan that's 3 inches deep, tapping out the excess flour.
* In a small saucepan, melt the butter and brown sugar together, stirring until smooth. Pour the mixture into the cake pan and swirl it to cover the bottom.
* Sift flour, baking powder, baking soda, salt, ginger, cinnamon, and cloves into a medium bowl. Set aside.
* In a large bowl, cream the butter and sugar together until light and fluffy. Set aside.
* Using a fork, stir 1 teaspoon of the baking soda vigorously into the molasses, until the molasses has lightened, about 1 to 2 minutes.
* Add the molasses to the creamed butter and sugar then mix until fully combined.
* Stir in the flour.
* Stir in the water; mix until just smooth. Finally add the eggs one at a time, mixing thoroughly each time. The batter will be very thin.

✳ Pour the batter into the prepared pan; bake until a toothpick comes out clean, about 1 hour and 15 minutes.

✳ Cool 5 minutes, then invert the cake onto a serving plate. Allow the cake to cool, but serve warm.

✳ Just before serving sauté the apples over medium heat with the butter and sugar. Allow the apples to cool slightly, then top the cake with the warm apples and serve with whipped cream.

Carrot-Banana Cake

Cake:

2 cups all-purpose flour
1 tablespoon ground cinnamon
2 teaspoons baking soda
$^1/_4$ teaspoon salt
1 cup vegetable oil
1 cup sugar
1 cup firmly packed light brown sugar
4 large eggs
$1^1/_2$ cups finely grated carrots
1 cup drained crushed pineapple in juice
$^1/_2$ cup mashed ripe banana
$^3/_4$ cup chopped pecans

Frosting:

1 8-ounce package cream cheese, room temperature
1 cup powdered sugar
3 tablespoons unsalted butter, room temperature
$^1/_4$ teaspoon ground cinnamon
Additional ground cinnamon for garnish

Cake:

* Preheat oven to 350°. Grease and flour a 9 x 13-inch pan.
* Sift the first four ingredients into a medium bowl.
* In a large bowl, whisk the eggs, then whisk in the oil, sugar, and brown sugar until well blended.
* Stir in the flour mixture.
* Add the carrots, pineapple, banana and pecans and blend well.
* Transfer the batter to the prepared pan. Bake until a tester inserted near the center of the cake comes out clean, about 1 hour.
* Leave the cake in the pan on a rack for 10 minutes, then remove it from the pan and cool completely.

For the frosting:

* Beat all ingredients in a medium bowl until smooth. Frost and sprinkle with cinnamon when done.

Chocolate Decadence Pie Serves 8

*A tip for melting
chocolate:*

*I often remove the
chocolate from the heat
before it's fully melted
and let the residual
heat melt it the rest of
the way; it speeds up
the cooling process.*

One of my mess cooks dubbed this the "If-you-aren't-going-to-eat-that-then-I-will Pie". I mess around with the flavorings for this pie all the time.

2 8-ounce packages cream cheese, room temperature
2 squares unsweetened chocolate
$1^1/_2$ cups chocolate chips
$^1/_2$ cup half and half
5 eggs
$^1/_2$ teaspoon peppermint extract

Pie Crust:

2 cups crushed Oreo cookies
$^3/_4$ cup melted butter

Topping:

2 tablespoons sugar
$^1/_2$ cup whipping cream

* Preheat oven to 350.
* Heat the chocolate and half and half over a double boiler until the chocolate is melted; cool slightly. I will often remove the chocolate from the heat before it's fully melted and let the residual heat melt it the rest of the way. That way I don't have to wait as long for it to cool.
* Add $^1/_4$ of the melted chocolate to the cream cheese. Add a bit more and then the rest.
* Add the eggs and extract.
* Melt the butter and mix it with the Oreo crumbs, then press the mixture into the bottom and sides of a pie plate.
* Pour in the chocolate mixture and bake for about 30 minutes. It should still be a little wiggly in the center when you take it out.
* While the pie is cooling whip the sugar and whipping cream together.
* Serve with a dollop of whipped cream.

Variation:
*Replace the peppermint extract with cinnamon or almond
extract.*

Fresh Lime Pie

2 cups graham cracker crumbs
2 tablespoons sugar
$^1/_2$ cup (1 stick) unsalted butter, melted
14-ounce can sweetened condensed milk
$^1/_2$ cup freshly squeezed lime juice
2 large eggs, separated
$^1/_2$ teaspoon vanilla extract
1 tablespoon sugar

* Preheat oven to 325°.
* Mix the graham cracker crumbs, sugar and melted butter together in a medium bowl.
* Press the mixture into an 8 or 9-inch pie pan and chill about 15 minutes.
* Bake until the crust is firm and crisp (about 10 minutes).
* In a medium bowl, combine the condensed milk, lime juice, egg yolks and vanilla and beat until smooth and thick.
* In a separate bowl, beat the whites until they hold soft peaks.
* Add the sugar to the whites and continue beating until stiff. Fold the whites into the lime mixture and turn into the prepared shell.
* Bake until the filling is set, about 15 minutes. Cool and serve.

Lemon-Thyme Pound Cake

1 cup sugar
$1^{1}/_{2}$ cups (3 sticks) butter, softened
8 large eggs, separated
1 tablespoon grated lemon rind
2 tablespoons lemon juice
1 teaspoon lemon extract
$^{1}/_{4}$ cup milk
2 cups unsifted bleached all-purpose flour (unbleached will make a heavy cake)
2 teaspoons baking powder
$^{1}/_{4}$ teaspoon salt
1 teaspoon cream of tartar
$^{3}/_{4}$ cup sugar
$^{1}/_{2}$ cup fresh whole lemon-thyme leaves (you can substitute regular fresh thyme if lemon-thyme is not available)

✳ Preheat oven to 325°. Grease and flour a bundt pan.
✳ In a large bowl, beat the sugar and butter together until smooth. Set aside.
✳ Separate the eggs, placing the whites in a separate large bowl and mixing the yolks into the sugar and butter mixture.
✳ Stir the lemon rind, lemon juice, lemon extract, and milk into the egg/sugar/butter mixture.
✳ Sift the flour, baking powder, and salt (NOT the cream of tartar) into the batter and beat in at low speed.
✳ Add the cream of tartar to the egg whites and whip until foamy. Add the sugar and beat until stiff peaks are formed.
✳ Gently fold the egg whites and thyme leaves into the batter.
✳ Spoon the batter into the prepared pan and bake for $1^{1}/_{4}$ to $1^{1}/_{2}$ hours; test with a toothpick.
✳ Invert the cake on a rack and cool in the pan.

Mom's Chocolate Cake

Makes 12 servings

Cake:

$^1/_2$ cup (1 stick) soft unsalted butter
1 cup sugar
1 large egg
3 squares unsweetened chocolate, melted
1$^1/_3$ cups all-purpose flour
1 teaspoon baking powder
1 teaspoon baking soda
$^1/_2$ teaspoon salt
1 cup freshly brewed coffee
1 teaspoon vanilla extract

Frosting:

$^1/_4$ cup ($^1/_2$ stick) unsalted butter, softened
1$^1/_2$ cups confectioner's sugar
1 teaspoon vanilla extract
1 large egg
4 squares unsweetened chocolate, melted

Cake:

✳ Preheat oven to 350°. Butter an 8 or 9-inch round cake pan.
✳ Beat the butter with the sugar in a large mixing bowl until creamy.
✳ Add the egg and beat until the mixture is light and fluffy.
✳ Stir in the melted chocolate.
✳ Sift the dry ingredients into a separate bowl.
✳ Whisk $^1/_3$ of the dry ingredients into the butter mixture, then $^1/_3$ of the coffee, repeating until the flour and coffee are gone.
✳ Stir in the vanilla.
✳ Pour the batter into the prepared pan and bake until a toothpick inserted in center comes out clean, about 25 minutes.
✳ Cool for 10 minutes, then run a knife along the edge of the pan. Turn onto a rack; cool completely. Put on a cake plate or platter.

Frosting:

✳ While the cake cools, beat the butter in a mixing bowl until creamy.
✳ Add 1 cup of sugar and beat until smooth.
✳ Add the vanilla and egg and beat until smooth.
✳ Add the chocolate and stir until smooth.
✳ Add more sugar, or a few drops of coffee or milk, if necessary, to make the frosting spreadable.

As an alternative, leave the cake in the pan and frost only the top. This simplifies storage and transport.

Pie Crust

Makes 2 crusts

From *A Taste of the Taber* Cookbook

2 cups all-purpose flour
1 teaspoon salt
$^3/_4$ cup shortening
$^1/_4$ cup ice cold water (or more)

* Combine the flour, salt, and $^1/_2$ cup shortening into a medium bowl; cut in well with a pastry knife.
* Add the remaining $^1/_4$ cup shortening; blend well again and add $^1/_4$ cup water and mix until dough pulls away from the bowl and forms a ball.

Mom's Pecan Pie

Makes 8 servings

4 large eggs
1 cup sugar
3 tablespoons all-purpose flour
1 cup dark Karo syrup
$^1/_2$ teaspoon salt
3 tablespoons melted butter
2 teaspoons vanilla extract
1 cup whole pecans
1 unbaked pie crust (above)

* Preheat oven to 350°.
* Whisk the eggs together in a medium bowl.
* Thoroughly beat in the sugar, flour, syrup, salt, butter, and extract.
* Stir in the pecans.
* Pour the filling into the unbaked pie shell and bake 40 minutes. It's done when the nuts are golden brown and the center jiggles just a tiny bit.

Other Goodies

Apple Crisp

Filling:

12 tart apples
1 cup sugar
$1/_2$ teaspoon cloves
1 teaspoon cinnamon
1 tablespoon plus 1 teaspoon lemon juice

Topping:

$2^1/_4$ cups all-purpose flour
1 cup plus 2 tablespoons ($2^1/_4$ sticks) butter
$1^1/_2$ cups sugar
$1/_4$ teaspoon salt

* Preheat oven to 400°.
* Peel, core, and slice the apples into $1/_4$-inch wedges; toss them with the rest of the filling ingredients and spread them evenly in an ungreased 9 x 13-inch pan.
* In a separate bowl, cut the butter into the flour until the mixture is coarsely blended. Mix the sugar and salt into the topping; mixture should be crumbly.
* Place the topping on top of the apple mixture and bake for 45 minutes or until the top is browned and the liquid in the apples is dark.

Pumpkin Cheesecake

1 cup crushed graham crackers
$1/_4$ cup melted butter
1 teaspoon cinnamon
2 8-ounce packages cream cheese
$3/_4$ cup sugar
2 large eggs
1 cup canned pumpkin
2 tablespoons all-purpose flour
$1/_8$ teaspoon salt
$1/_2$ teaspoon ground cinnamon
$1/_4$ teaspoon ground nutmeg
1/8 teaspoon ground cloves
1/8 teaspoon ground ginger

* Preheat oven to 325°.
* Thoroughly combine the graham crackers, cinnamon, and melted butter. Press the mixture into the bottom of a spring form pan.
* In a large bowl, beat the cream cheese until fluffy.
* Gradually add the sugar, then the eggs, one at a time, then the pumpkin.
* Sift the dry ingredients into the cream cheese mixture and mix well.
* Bake 45 minutes to an hour until the cake is firm around the sides but still soft in the center.

Bourbon Street Bread Pudding

This is one of my favorites – and I don't even like bread pudding!

Pudding:

Day-old French bread, sliced 1-inch thick, enough to cover the bottom of a 9-inch square pan.
$^1/_2$ cup (1 stick) butter
1 cup sugar
5 eggs
2 cups heavy cream
Dash of cinnamon
1 tablespoon vanilla
$^3/_4$ cup raisins

Bourbon Sauce:

1 cup sugar
1 cup heavy cream
1 tablespoon butter
Dash of cinnamon
$^1/_2$ teaspoon cornstarch dissolved in $^1/_4$ cup water
$^1/_4$ cup bourbon

✳ Preheat oven to 350°. Grease a 9-inch square baking pan.
✳ Arrange the sliced bread in one layer in the bottom of the pan. If there are large gaps cut some pieces to fit.
✳ Cream the butter and sugar together in a medium bowl.
✳ Add the eggs, cream, cinnamon, vanilla and raisins and mix well.
✳ Pour the mixture over the bread and let stand for at least 5 minutes.
✳ Turn the bread over and let stand another 10 minutes.
✳ Cover the pan with foil and place it in a larger pan filled halfway with warm tap water. Bake for 30 minutes.
✳ Remove foil and bake for another 10-15 minutes. The custard should still be soft when done.
✳ Remove the pudding from the oven and water and cool a few minutes.
✳ While the pudding is cooling, combine all the sauce ingredients **except** for the bourbon in a saucepan and bring to a boil. Continue to boil until the sauce has thickened so it coats the back of a spoon. Remove the pan from the heat and add the bourbon. Keep warm.
✳ Cut the pudding into squares and serve with the warm sauce.

Drop Strawberry Shortcake

1 quart strawberries washed and sliced
$^3/_4$ cup sugar

Shortcake:

2 cups all-purpose flour
$^3/_4$ teaspoon salt
1 tablespoon baking powder
3 tablespoons sugar
1 tablespoon grated lemon zest
$^1/_2$ teaspoon ground nutmeg
$^1/_4$ cup ($^1/_2$ stick) cold, unsalted butter
1 cup buttermilk

Whipped Cream:

1 cup cream
3 tb sugar
$^1/_2$ ts vanilla extract

✳ Preheat oven to 350°.
✳ Mix the sliced strawberries and sugar together in a large bowl and set aside for at least   hour (to allow the juice to develop).
✳ In a large bowl, whisk together the flour, salt, baking powder, sugar, zest, and nutmeg.
✳ Cut in the butter using a pastry knife or fingertips until coarsely mixed.
✳ Stir in the buttermilk until the mixture is just blended.
✳ Drop onto an ungreased baking pan and bake until lightly browned, about 12 minutes.
✳ When the biscuits are done, whip the cream, sugar, and extract.
✳ To serve, cut the shortcakes in half, spoon the berries on top of the bottom half of the shortcake, place the top half of the shortcake on the berries, and top with whipped cream.

Ginger Ice Cream

This recipe is in honor of a crew member who was with us for several years. He turned me on to ginger beer, although the one he likes will blow the back of your head off. THIS recipe has enough ginger in it!

$^1/_2$ cup sugar
$^1/_4$ cup coarsely grated peeled ginger root
2 tablespoons water
2 cups half and half
4 large egg yolks
1 cup heavy cream
1 teaspoon vanilla extract
$^1/_2$ cup coarsely chopped crystallized ginger

✳ In a medium saucepan, cook the sugar, ginger root, and water over moderate heat, stirring occasionally, for 5 minutes.
✳ Stir in the half and half and bring to a simmer, stirring often.
✳ In a separate bowl, whisk the egg yolks and gradually add the half and half mixture in a slow stream, whisking constantly.
✳ Pour the mixture back into the saucepan and cook over moderately low heat, stirring constantly, until a thermometer registers 170° (do not let boil).
✳ Pour the custard through a sieve into a clean bowl and stir in the heavy cream and vanilla.
✳ Cover the surface of the mixture with plastic wrap and chill until cold.
✳ Follow the instructions for your electric or hand-cranked ice cream maker.
✳ Add the finely chopped crystallized ginger $^3/_4$ of the way through the process.

Beverages

I've served all these recipes on board when the weather has taken a turn toward the foggy or the chilly. When we've got a group of school kids on board, I just keep a pot of hot cocoa going all the time – that is until the sugar level gets a bit high! Wassail is a drink that my mom serves every Christmas and I can't smell it without remembering family times. Chai tea is an Indian drink that has become popular in coffee houses. I found this recipe several years ago and it's a nice alternative to hot chocolate.

Warm, Flannel,
Homemade *Quilts*

*One of the special
touches we have on the
Riggin is homemade
quilts. Early into our
stewardship of the
Riggin, I realized we
needed new blankets for
the bunks in the cabins.*

*I love quilting and sewing
and it's something I'm
able to do in the
wintertime, so over the
course of two winters I
made quilts for each
bunk on the Riggin. They
all have rich, deep hues
and an abundance of
soft flannel to keep
everyone cozy during
crisp fall evenings.*

I make a batch of the spice base all at once so it's always available.

1 bag of tea (orange pekoe or your favorite)
1 teaspoon spice base (below)
1 cup milk
1 tablespoon sugar

✳ In a small saucepan, bring the water, tea bag and 1 teaspoon of the spice mix to a boil; remove from heat and steep approximately 5 minutes.
✳ Add the milk and sugar; return the pan to the stove over medium-high heat and continue to heat until the liquid is hot but not boiling. Serve immediately.

Spice base

4 tablespoons ground cinnamon or 8 sticks
2 tablespoons cardamom seeds (try to buy them without the pods. If they are in the pods, remove the pods and measure just the seeds)
1 teaspoon whole black peppercorns
8 whole star anise

✳ Grind the spice base ingredients together in a food processor or spice grinder until finely ground.
✳ You can store the mixture in an airtight container for months.

Hot Chocolate

I've found that this is a real treat for little ones when you use semi-sweet chocolate; grown-ups usually prefer bittersweet.

3 cups whole milk
3 ounces bittersweet or semi-sweet chocolate, finely chopped or grated

✳ Heat the milk in a saucepan over medium-high heat until it is just ready to boil.
✳ Put the chocolate in a blender and pour in the hot milk.
✳ Allow the mixture to sit for 10-15 seconds, so the chocolate begins to melt; cover securely, place a folded towel over the lid, and blend until completely mixed and frothy, about 30 seconds.
✳ Serve with marshmallows.

Wassail Bowl Punch

1 quart hot tea (black or orange pekoe, or your favorite)
1 quart cranberry juice
1 quart apple juice
2 whole cinnamon sticks
12 whole cloves
1 cup sugar
$^3/_4$ cup lemon juice
2 cups orange juice
1 orange, sliced
1 lemon, sliced

✳ In a large stockpot, combine all the ingredients except the orange and lemon slices.
✳ Bring to a boil, strain, and pour into a large bowl.
✳ Garnish with orange and lemon slices.

From the Pantry – Jams and Jellies

Some of my earliest memories are of canning jams, jellies, tomatoes and beans with my mom and grandma during our yearly visit to my grandma and grandpa's rural New York home. To my mind one of life's greatest pleasures is slathering a warm, freshly made slice of bread – Anadama, Crusty Peasant bread or Whole Wheat Walnut – with the bright taste of jam or jelly. My favorites are the ones that you don't cook for long. Their shelf life is not as long as others (no problem in our house) but the flavors are really as ripe as they can be.

Nectarine Jam

This jam shouldn't be canned due to the lower amount of sugar.

1 pound nectarines, peeled, pitted and sliced thin
$1^1/_4$ cups sugar
2 tablespoons fresh lemon juice

✳ Bring all the ingredients to a boil in a non-reactive skillet.
✳ Reduce heat and simmer until it begins to look syrupy. Skim off any foam that develops on the surface.
✳ Cool and serve.
✳ It will keep in the refrigerator for two weeks, or you can freeze it.

Plum Preserves

This jam shouldn't be canned due to the lower amount of sugar.

1 pound ripe, juicy plums, unpeeled, pitted, halved and thinly sliced
1 cup plus 2 tablespoons sugar
2 tablespoons lemon juice

✳ Bring all the ingredients to a boil in a non-reactive skillet.
✳ Reduce heat and simmer until it begins to look syrupy. Skim off any foam that develops on the surface.
✳ Cool and serve.
✳ It will keep in the refrigerator for two weeks, or you can freeze it.

Red Pepper Jam

2 large red bell peppers, seeded and finely chopped
$1^1/_2$ teaspoons kosher salt
$^3/_4$ cup cider vinegar
$1^1/_4$ cups sugar

* Place the peppers in a large bowl, sprinkle them with the salt, and let them sit for 30 minutes.
* Drain the excess liquid.
* Rinse the peppers in cold water and drain the water; rinse and drain again.
* Put the peppers into a wide, heavy saucepan with the vinegar and sugar.
* Bring the mixture to a boil and stir for 15-20 minutes or until the peppers are translucent and the candy thermometer reads 220 degrees.
* Ladle the jam into hot sterilized jars and seal. Refrigerate up to 2 months or freeze for up to a year. If you're freezing them leave additional space in the jars.

Sour Cherry and Black Raspberry Jelly
Makes about eleven 6-ounce jars of jelly

2 pounds ripe sour cherries, thoroughly washed but not pitted
1 quart black raspberries, washed
$^1/_2$ cup water
$7^1/_2$ cups sugar
1 bottle Certo
1 teaspoon butter
$^1/_4$ cup paraffin, melted

* Do not pit, but crush the cherries.
* Grind or crush the black raspberries.
* In a large saucepan, combine the fruits and water. Bring to a boil and simmer, covered, for 10 minutes.
* Place in a jelly cloth or bag and squeeze out the juice.
* Measure sugar and $3^1/_2$ cups of the juice in to a large saucepan and mix. Bring it to a boil over high heat; add the Certo all at once, stirring constantly.
* Bring to a full rolling boil and boil hard for 30 seconds.
* Remove from heat, skim off any foam, and pour quickly into sterilized jars.
* Immediately pour about $^1/_4$-inch of paraffin in each jar.
* Allow the paraffin to set before putting lids on the jars.

Rhubarb-Orange Marmalade

Makes 2 cups

5 cups sliced rhubarb (-inch slices)
$^1/_4$ cup cold water
3 cups sugar
1 package orange gelatin mix

* Put the rhubarb and water in a large saucepan; cover, bring to a boil, then reduce heat and steam until tender.
* Stir in the sugar; reduce heat to low and cook 8 minutes, stirring occasionally.
* Remove from heat.
* Add the dry gelatin; stir well.
* Ladle into sterilized jars and seal.

Strawberry Jam

Makes 5 cups

3 pints strawberries
$2^1/_2$ cups sugar

* Wash the berries and remove the hulls.
* Pour about $^1/_2$ cup of sugar in the bottom of a 3-quart pot. Cover with $^1/_3$ of the strawberries. Repeat 2 times, and cover with the remaining sugar.
* Cover the pot and set aside until all the sugar is absorbed (about 3 hours)
* Bring the berries to a boil over high heat, stirring occasionally.
* Reduce heat to medium and cook, uncovered, for 20 minutes, stirring frequently.
* When the mixture is syrupy and thick remove it from the heat, skim off any foam, and pour quickly into sterilized jars.
* Immediately pour about $^1/_4$ -inch of paraffin in each jar.
* Allow the paraffin to set before putting lids on the jars.

Composting at Sea

Below is an excerpt from a "Best Practices" collection prepared by MEBSR, Maine Businesses for Social Responsibility.

There are several barriers to composting and recycling on board a schooner, not the least of which is limited space. This is especially true for boats that do longer trips, such as the J.&E. Riggin. In addition, compost smells and can attracts bugs – a problem which is intensified again by the limited space.

In their efforts to operate a business that has a low impact on the environment, the owners of the J.&E. Riggin found a way to compost and recycle on board their weeklong sailing trips. They use 5 gallon buckets with snapping lids to store the organic compostable materials. And since the buckets are stored on deck, this also eliminates the potential problems of smell and bugs. The practice requires some education of guests on what can and cannot go into the compost (no dairy/meat products, only vegetable matter). But the owners have found that the guests enjoy learning about composting and where the compost goes (which is back into the owner's garden where some of the herbs used on board are grown). The owners have also found that this knowledge helps the guests feel more grounded about the business, as they are able to see how the owners are connected to the community. Recyclable containers are crushed and stored under the deck in an area they call the "lazarette."

There is a good deal of time investment that goes into recycling and composting, but Captain Anne Mahle believes the results have been worth it. The J.&E. Riggin has reduced its typical garbage load from 2-3 bags a day to 2-3 bags a week! In addition, the actual garbage, which is also stored below deck, doesn't smell as much because most of the organic materials that would otherwise decompose are separated and stored in the compost on deck.

Eco-Friendly Cleaning

When I first decided to try making my own cleaning supplies I wanted to find something as effective as the store bought products, but not as harmful. I could have simply purchased the eco-friendly products on the market, but I found they were prohibitively expensive. What you'll find in this chapter are the most useful, most effective recipes I've found to date. They smell better too!

These recipes are based on those found in **Clean and Green** by Annie Berthold-Bond. We've found these simple recipes to be very effective in keeping our galley and deck clean without adding anything harmful to the water.

Ten Dollars is Ten Dollars

One of the responsibilities of a deckhand on the Stephen Taber was "bucketing" down the deck. We would tossing a deck bucket attached to a long piece of rope over the side, haul up a bucket of seawater, and sluice the water over the deck. It was not uncommon for a deck bucket to be lost overside during this process. The rule was that the captains would pay for the first bucket lost over the side, but any others were on the crews' nickel.

My deckmate and I had already lost one bucket early in the season; we were determined to not forfeit one cent of our paychecks for another. One week I, with more enthusiasm than was warranted, tossed my bucket over the side. Before I knew it the rope slipped from my fingers. Without time to consider the freezing temperature of Maine's water, I jumped in after it. I got it – and applause from the passengers watching from the dry, warm, deck.

Fantastic Cleaner

Adapted from **Clean & Green** by Annie Berthold-Bond

1 teaspoon Borax
$^1/_2$ teaspoon washing soda (available in the detergent section of most grocery stores)
2 tablespoons white vinegar or lemon juice
$^1/_4$ to $^1/_2$ teaspoon vegetable oil-based liquid soap (i.e., Heavenly Horsetail All-Purpose Cleaner or Dr. Brunner's Soap)
2 cups very hot tap water
10 drops essential lavender oil
10 drops essential rosemary oil

✳ Measure all the ingredients into a clean, empty spray bottle and shake until everything is dissolved.
✳ The spray bottle makes this great for easy cleanups.

Floor Cleaner

From **Clean & Green** by Annie Berthold-Bond

2 tablespoons washing soda
2 tablespoons Borax
$^1/_4$ c white vinegar or lemon juice
1 tablespoon vegetable oil-based liquid soap
2 gallons very hot tap water

✳ Mix everything together in a soap bucket until the borax is dissolved.
✳ Mop and rinse.

Window Wash

From **Clean & Green** by Annie Berthold-Bond

3 tablespoons white vinegar or lemon juice
$^1/_4$ to $^1/_2$ teaspoon vegetable oil-based liquid soap (i.e., Heavenly Horsetail All-Purpose Cleaner or Dr. Brunner's Soap)
2 cups very hot tap water
Spray bottle

✳ Measure all the ingredients into a clean, empty spray bottle and shake until dissolved.

Low Fat, Low Carbohydrate, and Vegetarian Dishes

Low Fat

Breakfast & Brunch

Fruit Compote
Blueberry Syrup
Toasted Oatmeal

Appetizers

Green Olive Tapenade
Sun-Dried Tomato Spread

From the Garden

Banana Salsa
Black Bean Salad
Chicken, Roasted Red Pepper and Couscous Salad
Couscous and Chickpea Salad
Garbanzo Bean and Roasted Eggplant Salad
Lentil and Sun-Dried Tomato Salad
Melon and Israeli Couscous Salad
Roasted Beet and Goat Cheese Salad
Roasted Onions
Sautéed Greens

Soups

Bermuda Fish Chowder
Black Bean Chili
Black Bean Soup
Mushroom Barley Soup
Tomato Soup with Herbed Yogurt
Turnip and Leek Soup

Sides

Cinnamon Roasted Sweet Potatoes
Garlic Mashed Potatoes (replace the butter with olive oil)

Fish

Caribbean Spiced Fish
Pomeroy Mussels
Salmon with Tri-Pepper Salsa
Sesame Seared Tuna
Clam Sauce

Meat

Beef Ragu with Fennel and Orange

Braised Lamb Shanks with Thyme, Cinnamon and Fennel
Curried Lamb and Lentil Stew
Riggin Ham
Pork Loin Dinner with Cranberry Port Sauce

Poultry

Chicken And Winter Veggie Stew
Chicken Curry
Chicken Paprika
Cornish Game Hens with Smoked Shrimp and Brandy Stuffing
Roasted 5-Herb Chicken
Lemon Garlic Chicken
Rosemary Chicken And Dumplings
Grilled Chicken with Passion Fruit Sauce

Vegetarian

Puttanesca
Roasted Pine Nut and Eggplant Sauce

Yeast Breads

Anadama Bread
Crusty Peasant Bread
Focaccia
Jiffy Oatmeal Bread
Newfi Bread (Windjammer Fleet Recipe)
Sunflower Millet Bread
Whole Wheat Walnut Bread
Very Easy Bread Recipe

Biscuits, Quick Breads, and Muffins

Golden Northern Cornbread
Irish Soda Bread
Mom & Grandma's Brown Bread

Beverages

Wassail Bowl Punch

From the Pantry

Plum Preserves
Nectarine Jam
Red Pepper Jam
Rhubarb-Orange Marmalade
Sour Cherry and Black Raspberry Jelly
Strawberry Jam

Low Carbohydrate

Appetizers

Artichoke and Red Pepper Dip
Herbed Feta Cheese
Green Olive Tapenade
Lobster Dip
Salmon Dip
Sun-Dried Tomato Spread
Warm Cheddar and Horseradish Dip

From the Garden - Salads

Roasted Beet and Goat Cheese Salad
Roasted Onions
Sautéed Greens

Dressings

Blue Cheese Vinaigrette
Creamy Blue Cheese Dressing
Creamy Herb Dressing

Soups

Italian Sausage Soup
Spinach Gorgonzola Soup
Thai Red Curry Soup
Tomato Soup with Herbed Yogurt

Fish

Caribbean Spiced Fish
Curried Mussels
Haddock with Herb Butter over Caramelized Onions and Tomatoes
Clam Sauce
Pomeroy Mussels
Salmon with Tri-Pepper Salsa
Sesame Seared Tuna

Meat

Beef Ragu with Fennel and Orange
Black Forest Pork Stew
Bolognese Sauce
Braised Lamb Shanks with Thyme, Cinnamon and Fennel
Riggin Ham
Riggin Rib Roast with Horseradish Cream
Pork Loin Dinner with Cranberry Port Sauce
Sautéed Beef Tenderloin Steak with Port and Mushroom Sauce

Chicken

Chicken Curry
Chicken Paprika
Roasted 5-Herb Chicken
Lemon Garlic Chicken

Vegetarian

Breakfast & Brunch

Crepes Eggs Benedict (leave out the Canadian Bacon)
French Toast
Frittata

Appetizers

Artichoke and Red Pepper Dip
Herbed Feta Cheese
Green Olive Tapenade
Lemon-Pepper Cheese Crackers
Sun-Dried Tomato Spread
Warm Cheddar and Horseradish Dip

From the Garden –Salads

Black Bean Salad
Garbanzo Bean and Roasted Eggplant Salad
Lentil and Sun-Dried Tomato Salad
Melon and Israeli Couscous Salad
Roasted Beet and Goat Cheese Salad
Roasted Onions
Sautéed Greens

Soups

Black Bean and Jasmine Rice Soup
Mushroom Barley Soup
Spinach Gorgonzola Soup
Tomato Soup with Herbed Yogurt
Turnip and Leek Soup

Sides

Barley Risotto
Cheesy Potatoes
Cinnamon Roasted Sweet Potatoes
Garlic Mashed Potatoes
Goat Cheese and Dill Mashed Potatoes
Mom's Potato Casserole
Polenta
Potato Gratin
Potato Pancakes
Roasted Red Wine Potatoes
Rosemary Potatoes
Yorkshire Pudding

Entrees

Caramelized Onion And Gorgonzola Tart
Puttanesca
Roasted Mushroom and Artichoke Sauce
Roasted Pine Nut and Eggplant Sauce
Summer Vegetable Strata

Tomato, Leek And Brie with Linguini
Tomato, Mascarpone and Kalamata Olive Pasta

Local Sources

Agricola Farms
Mark Hedrich and Linda Rose
2282 Heald Hwy
Rte 17 at Clarry Hill Rd
Union, ME 04862
207-785-4018
veggies4u2@aol.com
http://www.iconacraft.com/ModernWife/garden.html

Appleton Creamery
Fresh and aged goat cheese
Caitlin and Bradley Hunter
780 Gurney Town Rd
Appleton, ME 04862
207-785-4431 (Cheese Order Hotline)
info@appletoncreamery.com
http://www.appletoncreamery.com/

Borealis Breads
Jim Amaral
PO Box 1800
Wells, ME 04090
207-641-8800
info@borealisbreads.com
http://www.borealisbreads.com

Curtis Custom Meats
1719 Camden Rd
Rt. 90
Warren, ME 04864
207-273-2574

Jess's Market
Fish and Seafood
118 S Main St
Rockland, ME 04841
207-596-6068
Fax: 207-596-7292
JESS@midcoast.com

Rock City Coffee Roasters
Rockland, ME 04841
207-594-5688
Fax: 207-594-5689
http://www.rockcitycoffee.com/

Bowden's Egg Farm
Dennis Bowden
155 Goshen Rd

Waldoboro, ME 04572
(207) 832-7016

Nervous Nellie's Jams and Jellies
598 Sunshine Rd
Deer Isle, ME 04627
1-800-777-6845 or 207-348-6182
Fax: 1-800-804-7698
jam@nervousnellies.com
http://www.nervousnellies.com/index.html

Stonewall Kitchen
Stonewall Lane
York, ME 03909
1-800-207-JAMS (5267)
guestservices@stonewallkitchen.com
http://wwwstonewallkitchen.com

Ducktrap River Fish Farm, LLC
Smoked Fish and Seafood
57 Little River Dr
Belfast, ME 04915
800-828-3825
smoked@ducktrap.com
http://www.ducktrap.com/drff_cu.php

The King Arthur Flour Company, Inc
133 Route 5 South
PO Box 876
Norwich, VT 05055
800-827-6836
www.kingarthurflour.com

Maine Businesses for Social Responsibility (MEBSR)
200 High St
Portland, ME 04101
207-338-8908
info@mebsr.org
http://www.mebsr.org/

Maine Organic Farmers and Growers Association (MOFGA)
PO Box 170
Unity, ME 04988
207-568-4142
Fax: 207-568-4141
mofga@mofga.org
http://www.mofga.org/

A Taste of the Taber
Ellen Barnes
www.stephentaber.com
800-523-2145

Photo Credits

Thanks to everyone that allowed me to use their photographs or recipes in this book, or helped test the recipes. All photos other than those listed below were taken by Frank Chillemi. Numbering of the photographs is by page then by order of the photograph going clockwise from the upper left hand corner of the page (eg 23-2 indicates the second photograph on page 23).

Denise Adams: 9-3

Dana Degenhardt: S1-2, S4-3, S5-6, S6-1, S6-3, S14-2, S15-5, 19-1, 28-1, 32-1

Diane Dench: S6-2

Ed Dench: 4-2, 9-4, 18-1, 28-2, and photo of Annie and Jon on the back cover.

John Devlin: 9-6

Victor Dmuchoski: S4-1

Ed Glaser: *Riggin* under sail on the back cover.

Susan Hickey: S2-1

Norm Lampton: S9-1, S9-4

Neal Parent: 21-1

Curt Pasfield: 9-5

Carol Slabinski: S6-4, S10-4, S10-1, S10-6

Neil Tischler: 14-1

Jim Willis: S3-4, S10-1, S10-5, S10-1, S11-1, S16-2, 7-1, 12-2

Photographer Unknown: S9-2, S10-3, S10-4, S14-1, 4-1, 17-1, 20-1, 20-2, 22-2, 23-1, 23-2, 27-2, 32-2, 32-3

Index

For more information, or to order cookbooks or free recipe cards,
please complete the card below and return to:

Schooner J&E Riggin
136 Holmes Street
Rockland, ME 04841

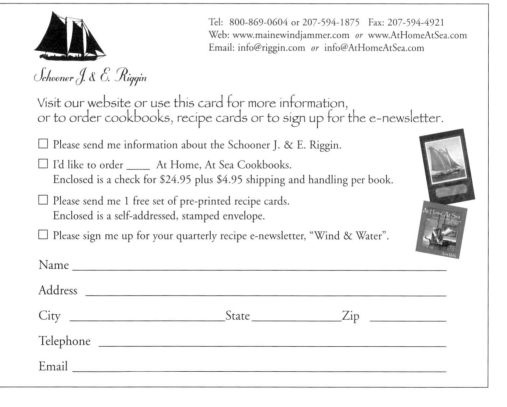

Tel: 800-869-0604 or 207-594-1875   Fax: 207-594-4921
Web: www.mainewindjammer.com *or* www.AtHomeAtSea.com
Email: info@riggin.com *or* info@AtHomeAtSea.com

Schooner J. & E. Riggin

Visit our website or use this card for more information,
or to order cookbooks, recipe cards or to sign up for the e-newsletter.

☐ Please send me information about the Schooner J. & E. Riggin.

☐ I'd like to order _____ At Home, At Sea Cookbooks.
 Enclosed is a check for $24.95 plus $4.95 shipping and handling per book.

☐ Please send me 1 free set of pre-printed recipe cards.
 Enclosed is a self-addressed, stamped envelope.

☐ Please sign me up for your quarterly recipe e-newsletter, "Wind & Water".

Name _____

Address _____

City _____ State _____ Zip _____

Telephone _____

Email _____